TODDLER DISCIPLINE

Behavior Problems and to Raise a Happy Child

(Fundamental Years With a Tailored Method for Every Age and Stage)

Heather Chung

Published By **Heather Chung**

Heather Chung

All Rights Reserved

Toddler Discipline: Behavior Problems and to Raise a Happy Child (Fundamental Years With a Tailored Method for Every Age and Stage)

ISBN 978-1-77485-440-2

All rights reserved. No part of this guide may be reproduced in any form without permission in writing from the publisher except in the case of brief quotations embodied in critical articles or reviews.

Legal & Disclaimer

The information contained in this book is not designed to replace or take the place of any form of medicine or professional medical advice. The information in this book has been provided for educational and entertainment purposes only.

The information contained in this book has been compiled from sources deemed reliable, and it is accurate to the best of the Author's knowledge; however, the Author cannot guarantee its accuracy and validity and cannot be held liable for any errors or omissions. Changes are periodically made to this book. You must consult your doctor or get professional medical advice before using any of the suggested remedies, techniques, or information in this book.

Upon using the information contained in this book, you agree to hold harmless the Author from and against any damages, costs, and expenses, including any legal fees potentially resulting from the application of any of the information provided by this guide. This disclaimer applies to any damages or injury caused by the use and application, whether directly or indirectly, of any advice or information presented, whether for breach of contract, tort, negligence, personal injury, criminal intent, or under any other cause of action.

You agree to accept all risks of using the information presented inside this book. You need to consult a professional medical practitioner in order to ensure you are both able and healthy enough to participate in this program.

TABLE OF CONTENTS

INTRODUCTION 1

CHAPTER 1: INFANT AND TODDLER DEVELOPMENT - LEARNING STARTS NOW! 5

CHAPTER 2: AGE-APPROPRIATE TODDLER DISCIPLINE STRATEGIES 23

CHAPTER 3: KEEPING A UNITED FRONT 31

CHAPTER 4: DISCIPLINE VS. PUNISHMENT 41

CHAPTER 5: UNDERSTANDING TODDLERS 51

CHAPTER 6: INSIDE THE TODDLER MIND 65

CHAPTER 7: HOW TO STOP TODDLER TEMPER TANTRUMS 79

CHAPTER 8: AN REMINDER FOR PARENTS 93

CHAPTER 9: POSITIVE DISCIPLINE 97

CHAPTER 10: DEVELOP COOPERATION, RESPONSIBILITY AND AFFECTION 116

CHAPTER 11: WHAT ARE THE STRESS FACTORS FOR CHILDREN? 129

CHAPTER 12: FOOD FIGHT 144

CHAPTER 13: THE HEALING POWER OF TANTRUMS 153

CHAPTER 14: DISCIPLINE WITHOUT SHAME 162

CHAPTER 15: THINGS YOU NEED TO CONSIDER WHEN DISCIPLINING TODDLERS 164

CONCLUSION 176

Introduction

The concept of toddler discipline is not negative. Instead, it teaches your child how the left brain works and helps you stop the right-emotional mind gaining control. You have learned two strategies that are both scrumptious. These include parental behavior and child development. Practical advice and examples will help you to handle specific situations.

It is vital that you know when to discipline your child. Is this just an expression of their feelings?

Here are some occasions when you might need to discipline your child.

Their actions could put them in harm's way: If your child approaches the stove and you tell them to stop, their natural instinct is to go for it. This could make them hurt and potentially put them in danger. Your goal with discipline is to help your child learn the difference between right actions and wrong actions. You should also take steps to discipline your child if they do continue to act in dangerous ways.

Your child's actions can put others in danger. If they are covering baby's faces with a pillow, playing with matches in her big sister's hair, or doing any other thing that could put another person in danger, it is time to send them home. It is essential that you explain to them why this is wrong. However, once they have been warned, you must continue with the punishment to ensure they don't hurt anyone else.

When they do something that causes harm to someone or anything: If they are running around the house they could hit something and break it, or knock into you. This can lead to the baby being dropped. To help them understand the importance of discipline, it is essential that you keep your promises to them when they cause harm to another person or thing.

They do not want to follow your instructions. For example, if you tell your child "Don't do it," and they immediately comply, that is direct disobedience.

Obedience is essential for their safety and that of others.

It is important to keep discipline in mind for important moments and not just punish your child because they are acting out. If the behavior is severe enough that it warrants discipline, you will not be spending all of your time punishing them.

Now you are equipped to provide the support your child requires. You can now implement the strategies in various situations, so you can ensure your tot is happy and healthy.

Instead of hoping that one lesson will work, remember the golden rules: listen, repeat and offer a solution. Your toddler is amazing. You should show respect for him/her in all that you do.

You have the power of shaping your child's future or causing harm to your child. You have to apply what you've learned by reading the information and using reverse psychology to keep your child learning and interested. These pages will help you continue to refer to the information as you need it, whether you want to instill moral values, respect and good ways or build confidence.

Enjoy this stage of your toddler's development. There are so many things that can be interesting, exciting, and entertaining. As your child matures, they will start to relax and not get into all the details, but they will still need your love, affection, and support. Even when you are in the throes or of great upset, love and respect are two things you should never withhold.

Chapter 1: Infant And Toddler Development - Learning Starts Now!

Your child will notice many changes at twelve months. Many are now able to walk and some can even run. Your youngster's receptiveness to information is improving. While your youngster may be beginning to understand many words, his ability to articulate them is not yet clear.

The Sensory Motor Stage, which is ordinarily between 0 and 2 years old, is the first phase in tyke progression. This stage allows a child to discover about his/her condition and self through motor/reflex activities. Did you also know that your child's cerebrum is approximately five centimeters tall during the first three months of life? Your tyke's formative achievements will be greater between now, and five years.

Here are some of these real achievements:

Net Motor Skills - Learning to use substantial numbers of muscles for slithering, running, walking, and jumping.

Fine Motor Skills. Learn how to eat, draw, hold pastels, and dress.

Language: Learning to communicate using their body, external appearances, and verbally.

Cognitive: Develop reasoning skills by using rationale and reason, recalling information, and taking care to resolve simple problems.

Social: How to make connections with children, adults, teachers and other family members.

It's time to learn!

Learning is possible in many formats. Your youngster is looking at you intently all around and will often mirror what your do or say.

An excursion on the market can offer a rich learning environment. Calling attention the letters on the grain case or asking your tyke to shade an organic product. This develops language and cognitive skill.

Continue to allow your child to draw uninhibitedly, as well as encouraging them to make shapes. Because new illustration is a sequence of methods, it's easier to understand how to draw the shapes of objects. Your kid will probably soon have a house with both a square or triangle.

Five ways your toddler can learn to speak: Not-So-Terrible Twos

Toddlerhood can be a difficult time for child development. The infamous stages include frequent falls, fits, fits of anger, potty training, and the terrible two's. The baby months offer a wealth of opportunities. It is important to remember that babies are only babies for a few months. It's a crucial time block that can take up half of the initial 3 years. This isn't the time to let guardians down. It's a chance that your child can flourish!

Language blast is a crucial period in child development. Syntax and vocabulary are combined into a beautiful background that transforms infants into children, at least for the short-term.

Without expressive language dominance, a little child can be a parent's worst nightmare. It can be as crucial as a child who is not able to communicate what they need to you. The universe of special needs training has been explored. We have discovered some traps to help expand a child's initial capacity to communicate. Here are some suggestions!

Gesture-based communication

Baby communication using gestures is often referred to as a supernatural occurrence specialist. It can be used to teach babies as young as four month old how to sign "more,"'milk, and "hurt". Consider a scenario where ownership of rights was not transferred to you. It's not too late. Begin with a few vital signs. They will be more likely to follow your lead and use these signs every day. What if your child was able to request a snack or drink rather that dumping their bodies on the ground? You might find your child has something you don't understand. But sustaining the situation would be helpful. It's here and it is sufficiently understood.

Displaying Language

When you have children, it is not easy to talk with yourself. Talking to your child, regardless of how direct or indirect, about what you're doing shows that language encourages us all to think critically and make informed choices. Writing is an excellent way to build relationships. Your child may say, "We will get dressed now!" Let's finish. Expanding consistency in a child's day can decrease nerves, and even make them happier.

To begin with,

We use these ideas most often in our everyday life, but every once in awhile we talk about what happens next. Children often conceal what we tell them, just like their model. Use time request words like "First, we'll tidy up, and then we will have a bite" to show your child that you can take care of multiple requests. Now imagine your child needs to go on the playground. Now imagine your child lying on the floor, not taking off his coat or shoes. At this point, you will say "First, we get on our shoes. After that, we'll go the playground." This is an important asset.

Language Cards

The use of cards to enlarge a child's vocabulary may help them learn a language they are not fluent in. Simple cards that a child may choose and then hand to you in order to make a decision about sustenance, action, or any other variable. This completes the cycle of correspondence.

I like what I have

There are many options to include language in your conversations with your child if you think about them. You can also loan him your language. So, as you make him breakfast, you can tell him that you like grains. I'd like to have more. Next, if he is getting agitated, say it without much effort: "I need you to take me to the playground mom!" You will be able to help him settle down and start to accept the message.

As your child begins to grow out of infancy, and into the hectic, difficult, long period of toddlerhood it is important to place language at the top. Being able to help the person you are helping understand and use language can improve your parenting experience and your relationship.

Jigsaw Puzzles: Great for Toddler Growth

You will find many amazing age-appropriate jigsaws for your kid. Learning puzzles and jigsaws help to improve thinking and engine abilities. Puzzle play can be a fun and educational activity for little children. They are an excellent learning tool that can be used by children. Children can benefit from them if they are carefully considered. Here are some helpful tips for solving puzzles with your child.

Combining small puzzles with larger ones creates an interest in the critical thinking skills that jigsaws puzzles offer. Most children enjoy learning new things together with their parents. It's an incredible way to spend time with your children one on one. You might begin by explaining to your baby how to assemble the pieces. Then your child may follow your lead and in the end you may do it individually.

There are some simple, yet effective, puzzle options for young children that use board puzzles to help them learn. It's important to discuss the problem with your child and recognize pieces. This will encourage early reading and letter/number recognition. A few issues can help with various territories, such topography, reading the clock, finding information about life structures and nursery rhymes.

If your child does not seem interested at first, do not lose heart. It may take a while before the intrigue and ability develops. If your child has successfully completed the puzzle several times, you might want to turn it around so they don't get too bored. Many guardians might also pass puzzles on to their children and help them to solve the problem. It is better to keep them in a safe place and to encourage children to quickly put them away after playing.

As your child learns and develops, you will find new options that can help expand learning or advance existing skills. You can also use puzzles with your child's favorite TV character or hobby.

How Toddler Activities are Important for Child Development

The brain of a young baby is frequently compared to delicate, flexible dirt. Impressive and open. Many neural pathways have yet to be established in infanthood and early childhood. These will have an impact on how your child interacts to the planet and performs.

The toddler period is critical for child growth. This is vital because there are many toddler activities that will stimulate the brain.

You can either tell your toddler to stop watching TV or limit the amount of time they spend in front it. Television can stimulate the brain but it encourages no creativity, communication, action or creative energy. There are also proofs that it may cause issues with hostility. This is because the brain is addicted to the TV and this causes stagnation in sound learning and advancement.

Imagination

The imaginative process is essential for child growth. Your child will learn how to think creatively and develop their sense of self. They will also be able to discover their unique style and build their confidence. You can also use artistic interests to improve engine control. Your toddler can be encouraged by giving you tools. It is possible to use any type of material to create something. These could include colored pencils (finger paint), development paper, and markers. Also, you can do a round looking for examples and shapes in things such tiles, wood grain mists, shadows, and other materials.

Thinking

It is important to encourage your toddler's thinking abilities at the age they begin eating on their own. It's possible to find nourishment in a range of sizes, colours, and shapes. You might see your child arrange their foods in an intelligent manner. Your child's brain might be developing similitudes and contrasts.

Many guardians have been confused by the constant stream in which their toddler explains what's happening. This is, however, one of the best ways to show thinking abilities. You should respond honestly to their inquiries as best as you can. If you don't have any idea, be honest. If you confess that something isn't clear, it shows your child that nobody can be trusted.

Language

It is vital that your child has the ability to communicate in order to be able function in the public sphere. The earlier they learn, the better. Talking to your toddler is a great activity. You can also read to them, have them chat and play name games. This allows them to recite the names for arbitrary items. You can reward your toddler with applause if they react correctly.

Investigation

Children love to explore the world and are curious. Encourage your toddler's curiosity and exploration. They'll find endless things that are interesting to them. If you are interested in cultivating, your child can assist you by directing the worms/bugs to a protected area. These activities will help your child become more familiar and knowledgeable about the earth.

Fun Activities for Toddlers, Which Improve Their Development

It is something that many parents don't understand, but the toys that their toddlers play with can make a big difference in their toddler's development. For brain development, everything a young child does for the first two or three long periods of life is important. There are many exciting activities for toddlers to help your child develop. The brains of toddlers process a staggering amount of information. It is important for parents to provide formative toys for their children. Consider all the toys that are out there. There are many with bright colours, loud clamors and different surfaces. This is because toddlers need familiarity with different shades. Their brain development is stimulated by having them play with toys.

Toys that children use to improve their skills and learn how to build are soft toys and building squares. Because your child will discover that there are different sizes of building obstacles, you will need to provide them with a range of sizes. Additionally, playing with elastic balls is a wonderful learning tool. It allows your child to discover about other shapes and see how they function. In this early stage of your child's development, it is vital to give your child as many diverse toys and completed toys as possible. This will allow your child to express themselves creatively when they play.

Additionally, it is important to include melodic toys in toddler improvement. This is essential in encouraging enthusiastic insight in your toddler. These toys can stimulate their brains by playing new tunes. You can do this with toys and even instructive network TV shows. You can then move your child onto solving riddles, and even coordinating recreations as they become more proficient. This will make it easier for them to interact and create the neuron orders that your child needs for a great rest. This is an important part in childhood learning.

While there are many options for TV and PC entertainment, many people believe traditional toys are best suited to toddler development. Because it expects them only to play with one thing for a prolonged period of time. Children may become distracted and lose track of the important message when watching TV. Many people believe children will be able to improve their listening abilities and enhance their centering ability if they play with standard toys. Be mindful of the learning factor whenever you shop for toys for toddlers. There are many exciting activities available to your child.

Parenting Tip-Teddy's Discipline Book for Learning Good Parenting Skills

It can be difficult to successfully discipline your toddler. You will find the absolute best child-rearing advice toddlers discipline methods that have been tried and tested in this section.

Toddlers can be extraordinarily fun. Your curious nature and ability to learn and adapt to new situations will be unmatched. However, if your toddler gets into something that could cause harm or injury to someone or something else, you need to direct and apply toddler discipline. Some guardians may be annoyed at their youngster if they see such a situation. The majority of us will soon realize that such behavior won't get the response you seek.

As a method of reprimanding or warning your youngster, you can get him to start using this strategy. He will also learn how to shout to others so that they are noticed enough to get what they need. This isn't something that most guardians would want for their youngster.

Instead of shouting, try to tone down your voice. This will attract their attention, as they will need time to process what you are saying.

If you raise your voice, it will cause the kid to be scared. Imagine how you feel if someone shouts at and yells at. Just let your voice go and say "No!" This will help you achieve your goal.

If the toddler resists, lower your voice and repeat your order of "No!" Take a look at your toddler, and don't hesitate to say "No!"

In simple terms, inform them why they are unable to inspect that area or go ahead with the conduct. It will consume their bodies, so communicate it to them.

"Doing so will enable your toddler's understanding to be reinforced and allow them to feel as if they are able to investigate their condition.

Another unique tip for toddlers in child-rearing is not to take their conduct too literally. Every now and then, toddlers will begin to voice their opinions and will lash out at family members and friends.

You are not the only parent who is struggling to get your child to fit.

This is their way of testing your limits, your strengths, and understanding. How you handle these fits can affect how your child will request things later on in their lives.

Being a parent is the most horrible thing that can happen. To allow your child to have their way through fits of rage, it will teach them that they can continue to do what is right if they need.

To make a toddler behave, the best child parenting tip is to ignore them. Assure your toddler will behave well and avoid any mischief.

You can offer both negative and positive rewards to your child. It is important to not give in, regardless how humiliated.

Multi-day parenting can be difficult. Adapting to toddlers is not easy. However, you can make progress by addressing these issues.

Chapter 2: Age-appropriate Toddler Discipline Strategies

Have you ever been in deep discussions with your 2--12-month-old child over whether her princess dress will be worn to preschool for 5 consecutive days? You've probably had to remove the "stroll-of-shame" from your local grocery stores after your little one started throwing a tantrum. You may find consolation in knowing you're not alone. However, that doesn't make it easier to navigate your first years of life. The time when children begin to be more independent and develop their personalities is when toddlerhood can be particularly stressful for father and mother. But they still have a constrained capacity to talk and motive. Claire Lerner who is a child expert and director for parenting sources at the non-profit company zero to 3, says, "They know that their actions count -- it's up to them to make matters happen." This motivates them to put their stamp on the world, and to assert themselves in a manner that was not possible when they were young. They have very limited mental strength, and they may not be able think rationally now. It's not an easy combination. Here are some toddler discipline methods that can make it easier for your whole family to live together.

Be consistent

Lerner states that order, ordinariness and routine provide children with a refuge from the overwhelming and unpredictable world outside of their home. Children will feel safer and more comfortable when there is predictability and normal. This helps them to be calmer and better behaved because they know what they should expect. Keep the same time table every day. This includes having consistent nap, meal, and bedtimes.

Avoid stressful situations

Once your toddler is at toddler age, you have been able to spend enough time with them to be able recognize their triggers. They include hunger, sleepiness, and brief adjustments to venue. These situations are easily avoided with some planning. It is important that your child stays home during naptimes. Bedtimes are also important. For those times when you are away, keep food on hand for a quick hunger attack. Avoid making long trips. If you don't like the wait time at your chosen restaurant, try another one or shop elsewhere. You should plan accordingly so that you do not rush, especially when your infant needs to go to preschool. It is possible to ease transitions by talking with your infant. You could set up an egg clock for 5 mins and tell your baby to come get dressed when it has finished. It may be as simple as telling your baby that you prefer the blue blouse or the purple blouse for school. It is important to speak out loudly and have your child replace you about the next item on the timetable. Babies can comprehend a lot more that they can express.

Think like a Toddler

It is not the case that toddlers are mini-adults. They have trouble information on all the matters we ignore, including how to adhere to guidelines and behave correctly. A tantrum can often be avoided by seeing the situation from the perspective of an infant. While it is necessary to put a restriction in place, it is also important that you respect the child and use the occasion to help them cope with their frustrations. "Giving picks means you're able to identify your toddler and learn from their emotions. Asking your toddler to bring along a favorite e book inside the car or a snack can make it seem like he or her has some control.

Do the Art Of Distraction

Use your toddler's very short attention span to make it work for you. You can redirect your baby to a better activity like swapping the baby's ball for a book and/or moving the game out the door. Children need to be in an environment that encourages good behavior. If they get into something they didn't intend to, it's not necessary to punish them. However, you can give them a hobby or take them out and place them in another space.

Give your child a break

Time-outs may be one of the most important tools in the toddler world, but they are not an ideal approach for children. Children can learn to think that being sent away is bad and not good. You should not call it "time out", which can be confusing to children below 3, but instead, seek positive advice. Lerner recommends that your child create a comfortable corner, a safe space free from distractions and stimulation. This will allow them to relax for a few moments until they feel more in control. This helps you to recover as well. Be firm in correcting bad behavior but be sure to also praise good behavior. "If you do not tell your child that they are doing the correct factor, it is possible for them to take an interest in the wrong part. You can increase the likelihood that your child will return to something you have completed if it is explained to him or her.

Be calm

Your blood stress will quickly reach the boiling point as you watch your child throw a tantrum. It will make things worse. Give yourself some time for a break. "In all other cases, you are venting anger. It is going to make your experience of guilt and suffering worse. It will not do any good for your infant. In the event that you do provide your toddler with a time-out for any reason, be sure to limit it to only a few minutes or at this age. Children under three may find it confusing to call it time-out. Lerner suggests creating "cozy nooks," safe areas that are free of distractions and stimulation. Your baby can then simply relax in this area for a few moments until they get back on the right track. It is time to regroup.

While it is important to be accurate about reprimanding those who are doing the wrong thing, it is also important to make an effort not only to punish them but also to encourage good behavior. If you fail to notify your child when your child is doing the right things, they may just try the unsavory thing once in while trying to focus. You should inform your child that your child has accomplished something valuable. If they don't, there is a great chance your child will try it again. If you do give your child a time-out for doing something, be sure to limit it to no more than one minute. Talk about it as something much more than a timeout. Lerner suggests creating "secure nooks," safe areas that are free from stimulation and distractions. Your toddler can then kick back for a few more minutes until he/she feels like they have control. This helps you to recover. Don't be afraid to correct poor behavior. However, it is important to take the time and reward good behavior. It is possible for your toddler to want to do something again, even if you are telling them that they have done it correctly.

Know when it is time to say "No"

Positive things in a young child's life cannot be negotiable. She must eat, brush, and drive in a car. She has to take a shower once in a while. It's not acceptable to bit and hit. The hassles of controversy and multiple problems are not worth it. Pick your battles. "You need to decide whether or not it is worth fighting about. In the majority of cases, it isn't worth it to prevent it from happening. You can allow your son's superhero costume to be worn to the grocery or to read The Giving Tree at least 10 times per day. Once your child gets what they want, you can get him to switch to another option. For instance, he may choose to wear a different outfit or select a new book to study. Accept that your toddler may occasionally get a bit too much. "Remember, no one mother or father is perfect. But we try our best to make the most of every day. There will always be days when we're better at this than other times. "But if you figure continuously and have steady rules, you'll see more good days than bad ones.

Chapter 3: Keeping a United Front

Toddlers can be geniuses. Children learn very early that sometimes one parent is wrong and the other is right. This miscommunication between you as well-meaning partners can provide an opportunity for your fast-learning toddler, regardless of whether they want a candy bar or a skip bath, to get what it is that they want.

They discover who the easy victim is, and then they try to play you. Mom will always say yes and Dad will refuse. Jen and I noticed that our two-year old asked one of us for something. Then, he stopped asking the other.

It works when it does

After being duped repeatedly by our toddler, we now have an established family rule in which Mom and Dad should answer as one. It doesn't matter who you ask, as long as they both answer the same way. Although we may disagree on the subject behind closed doors, the person who gives the answer is our support. The second rule of this rule states that once your toddler has reached the age where they can understand the question, they must not ask any other parent.

It Doesn't Work When it Doesn't Work

The only reason this strategy doesn't work is if your partner and you really don't agree on something. More times than not, we've seen ourselves moving to another room and texting one another while waiting with baited breath for the outcome.

There are many silly things that your partner and you will disagree on. The things that seem big to one parent may not be important to the other. "Go to your Mom" or "Go to your Dad" will not work. This generally pivots your child to always go with the parent who will say "Yes."

Teamwork

The task of disciplining your toddler shouldn't be done alone. It would be easier to make it a team effort. Discuss any behavioral issues that you see in your child with the whole family. Include your child in the discussion. The essence of teamwork is being open and loving your fellow human beings, regardless of their faults. Teamwork requires perseverance and not giving up no matter how difficult the times may be.

Bonding

It is not just about bonding with family members, it's also a great way to strengthen your child's character. Children display many negative traits when they are upset, frustrated, or neglected. Families can bond better when they are close. It is also a way to express your love clearly. Children who are able to spend regular time with their family have more positive characteristics than kids who do not. They also tend not to lose sight of the importance of family ties as they grow older.

There are many different ways to bond with family members. You don't even have to travel far to bond with your loved ones. Your garden is a great place to play games and have a picnic. You can also ask your child if they would like to help with the cooking. Bonding is great. It is one the best things you could do.

Routines you can rely on

A consistent routine establishes expectations in the subconscious. Toddlers will be able to do the right thing without thinking about it. If a child understands what's going to happen next, they're more likely than not to fight you.

They know they must follow a certain sequence to enjoy other activities. They must do the same when they return home from school. After lunch, lunch boxes are placed on the counter. Backpacks and shoes are put in the bin. We're close to reaching the point where they do all of this without even needing to be reminded!

It works when it is

When we create a designated area for the children that stores all their school and school supplies, we can count upon them to place their items away once they return home from school.

When it doesn't work

When friends and family visit for several days or more, it is easy to interrupt even the most routine. If we're home, we tell guests what we expect (e.g. our kids should eat their dinner and have popsicles later).

Communication

Communication is key to any good relationship. By communication, I mean both speech and actions. You may not be speaking clearly to your children, but they will hear you speak. If we don't communicate what we want to see with our toddlers, it's difficult to place expectations. Your toddler will eventually understand that if your expectations have been met, it's better than if they don't. The four pillars are the foundation of a language your child can understand. You may experience tantrums, but that's normal.

Accepting their Feelings

Half of the battle lies in learning to accept your toddler's feelings. Realizing when it is okay to acknowledge their feelings and when it is best to keep them moving forward is half the battle. A quick hug, even if there is blood, works better than constant cuddling for toddlers who are hurt. It helps them learn to self soothe, which will be a key life lesson. We have a bunch of cartoonish bandages. However, we teach them to use their own self-help skills.

It works when it does

For Evelyn, a two-year old toddler, acceptance is key. However, she's still struggling to grasp the concepts possession and ownership. Lately she has started to adopt favorite toys she considers her own, along with a small purse that looks like an icecream cone. If she spots someone else with her iPhone (my older deactivated one), or her ceiling fan remote, she will start throwing a fit until the object is safely returned to her hands.

I could give "her", the toddler, the remote control back if she gets too excited (and I eventually do), but this would be taking advantage of an opportunity. I begin to calm her down by sitting with my daughter alone. Even though I don't fall into baby talk, I soften my voice. Accepting the stormy emotions shows them they might only be two, but they are still being heard.

When you consider their wishes, it shows that you value their individuality and respect them. It's also a way to build a relationship that allows for open communication. This skill will serve you well as they get older.

It's Not Working

Young toddlers do not understand how to play together, share or distinguish "good" feelings from "bad". They won't be able to understand the importance of positive interactions until they become more mature.

We parents are constantly learning. We teach our children to share all things, but sometimes it's okay to just have "yours." Charlie's second birthday party saw him receive a new water float. Charlie turned down the request of another little boy to have a turn, but he said no. While it was difficult for him to say, it was true. We were embarrassed by the situation and asked Charlie to let Charlie's friend play with it. It was almost as though the other child thought he was cheating us. He ran off with his friend.

Low, lower, lowest: How to get down on your level

This tool will allow you to reduce your size. Think of yourself as a toddler. Wouldn't it feel overwhelming to have to be talked to all the time by an adult? Although my 40-something knees groan, I always try to physically get down on their levels. It pays great dividends to keep them seated cross-legged or to hold their hands and connect eye-to eye. This simple strategy will allow your child to know that you are listening. Feeling heard is always a positive thing for toddlers.

It works when it works

I can't even count the number of times I have looked behind just once to see complete devastation. I learned to keep my cool, no matter if Ava was trying to smear baby lotion everywhere on the walls or to put talcum powder on my nightstand. I stopped, caught my breath, and sat down onto the floor. I kept eye contact with Ava as I explained why I was wiping lotion on the walls.

It doesn't always work

This is my Swiss Army Knife of tools. It can be used almost anywhere. If our children don't respond, it's often due to an underlying problem like fatigue or low glucose. When this happens, sometimes reasoning goes out of the window. I try to produce a different response after they've let their emotions go.

Communicating with action

Toddlers can be very busy, and they don't enjoy being interrupted. Sometimes, gentle movement is all they need to know you are paying attention. It could be as simple and as subtle as placing a hand on your head, shoulder or back. They will naturally be able to make eye contact, slow down and make eye contact when they feel the light touch.

When it Works

Toddlers aren't born knowing how they should clean up after themselves. So showing them what goes where and asking them if they want to do the same will give you far better results than simply asking. It creates a trusting moment between the two of them, and assures that they are doing a good job.

Charlie was three years old and would play with Dom his friend. He was so absorbed in his activities that it took him several times to look up, no mater how many times I repeated his name. The combination of making a request and placing my hand on his shoulder led to an immediate response.

Evelyn and me show Evelyn what it takes to be a good parent. Helping children learn simple tasks or how to clean up a place helps them grow. Give them lots of praise and encouragement when they do help.

It doesn't always work

Sometimes, the silent physical touch may not work. It's hard for them to use that type of physical communication if they've climbed into a fast food restaurant's playground. They might even be in a state of extreme overstimulation on Christmas morning or at a party.

Chapter 4: Discipline Vs. Punishment

It is important to note that punishment and discipline have different meanings. While punishment may have a punitive aspect, it does not change a child's behavior. In some cases, punishment can actually make the situation worse. The child doesn't learn, and only suffers. Punishment, unfortunately, can lead to humiliation of the child, significant discomfort, anger or more frustrations and anxiety.

On the other side, effective discipline can be both safe and beneficial for the child. While punishments are sometimes used in a discipline strategy that is effective, they are often mild and part of broader strategy. Last but not most, punishment is used to control a child. While discipline is used to guide a child, it allows him or her to learn from his mistakes.

Say no to spanking

While spanking may have been used in the past to discipline children, studies from today show that it does not work. Spiking can even worsen the situation. Spanking a toddler is a way to make him more aggressive. It does not teach him good behavior.

Spanking is motivated by pain. It's based on the belief that a person would cease doing harmful things. For example, if you touch the hot stove with your naked hand, you'll get burnt and need to be removed immediately. It sounds easy enough to discipline a child, but it is more complex than that. Discipline means telling your child what not to do and what to do. Discipline helps toddlers develop positive behaviors that lead to positive actions.

Another reason spanking can be harmful is the tendency for the child to lose faith in his parents. Your toddler can look up to your parents for support, comfort, or care. If you become a source to their pain, especially when it happens multiple times, your toddler will naturally try to put a shield around him. This causes a disruption in the parent/child relationship.

If you are a parent who uses spanking to discipline your child, it may be because you used to do so when you were younger, or perhaps because it was the best way for your child to behave. Here are five ways you can stop using spanking to discipline your child.

Learn to Use Words

Be more patient than physical aggression. Keep calm and avoid scolding. Make sure you use words your child can understand. Because toddlers don't have as much attention spans as adults, they aren't able to process as much information. Keep your words concise and easy to understand. Because you communicate through words, it is essential that you listen to your child. So that there is understanding, it should always be a two way conversation. It is more likely that there will be fewer issues if your child feels like you are listening. The same way you feel annoyed if your child can't understand your words, your child feels awful when you don't listen to them.

Shift from Focus

A shift in your focus can often be all that's needed. Instead of focusing on the negative, look at the positive. You can make it impossible for the negative to come out of your life if you only give all your attention to positive things.

Let him learn for himself

Experience is the best teacher, as they say. Your child can learn from his mistakes, but you don't always have to do it. Your toddler can learn from your actions by simply allowing the normal flow to happen. Your toddler may break his toy if he continues playing with it despite your warnings. This will teach your little one a valuable lesson. Of course, if your child is in danger, you need to immediately intervene and tell your child about the possible consequences.

Take a break

Give yourself a timeout. However, this time you should be the one to take the timeout. Don't lose your cool. Give yourself a break. For a moment, take a step back and try to cool your temper. Keep in mind that you should not confront your toddler if it is not calm and center. If you're in a public area and can't look away, it's best to pray for your child and keep your mind focused.

Be aware that spanking does not help

Multiple studies have proven that spanking is not the best way to discipline your child. The worst thing you can do for your child is spanking. Instead of spanking your children, consider positive and constructive ways you can correct wrong behavior.

Four Pillars of Effective Discipline

The best methods for disciplining a child are those that have four elements. These factors make them not only safe and healthful but also effective. The four pillars for effective discipline, unlike punishment, encourage learning and welfare in children.

It builds positive parent-child relationships

Effective discipline should complement the relationship between the child and parent. Effective discipline is not based on fear. It is based rather on understanding and love. Be aware that toddlers are highly sensitive. Their early childhood relationships have a profound impact on their brain and behavior. You can help your toddler develop positive relationships with other people. He will be able to learn the right conduct and also build a strong relationship of love, trust, and respect.

It's safe.

Safety is paramount for a child. Smart parents are against the use bodily hurt as a punishment. Sometimes, cruel punishments may be used against the child. Additionally, severe punishments may be inflicted if the parent loses his patience and is unable to control the situation.

It has reasonable expectations.

Discipline teaches your child good and appropriate conduct. Your expectations should be based on the child's brain development as well as their age. Positive behavior should be reinforced and encouraged. Negative behaviors should not be tolerated. Take note of any positive behavior your child displays, or at the very least try to.

It includes multiple techniques that are safe to use with the child.

A system or set of strategies that leads to effective discipline is called effective disciplining. Based on the circumstances, a certain technique will be used. This pillar again highlights the importance for safety. Every challenge behavior should not be considered a failure. It can serve as a learning experience that will allow the child to grow and learn. You as a parent must be able handle the situation calmly.

Is it really too late?

Some people believe that discipline is impossible for toddlers. You must remember that toddlers can experience rapid changes. Change is part and parcel of being a toddler. Either you change bad behavior to good behavior or you allow the bad behavior to continue. Of course, loving parents want the best for their child. If you are among those who feel that discipline is too late for your child, then you need to realize that it's never too late. Research shows that it is best to help your child become a happy toddler. You will have to make it harder for him to change his bad behavior when he becomes an adult.

But what if it doesn't?

Another problem most parents share is the fear of what happens if their child refuses to be disciplined. There are some points you need to be aware of. First, there are many methods that you can use for disciplining your child. First, you can't tell if it will work until you do something about it. Third, changing inappropriate or unsuitable behavior takes time. Fourth, toddlers are often capable of displaying multiple undesirable behaviors. At the very least, you can help him improve his bad habits with effective discipline. If you're fortunate enough, you might even be able fix his inappropriate behavior. Fifth, discipline is a way to help your child grow up as a person. Sixth, you can see that change does not just happen in toddlers; it also happens in adults. This means that there is no reason for you to assume that you can't change your child's behavior. At the very minimum, you can teach your child manners. Last but not less, it is your responsibility, as a parent and caregiver, to do all you can to help your child grow.

All children need boundaries. Boundaries are a great way to teach your toddler how to behave and they can also help him feel safe. The hard part about setting boundaries and making sure they are enforced is where the real challenge lies. This can be tricky, especially when you are trying to avoid coercing, threatening or coercing your children to listen to what you have to say. Set clear boundaries and be calm. This is a simple exercise which should be repeated over and over without any inconsistencies. There are no timeouts in parenting. It is all about the long-term.

Powerful emotions will set in when your child behaves badly or acts rudely. These situations are normal. Your emotional responses will influence the future conversation. Your body automatically switches into a fight or flee mode when your energy is low. This happens because your body is constantly flooded with adrenaline. These chemicals block your brain from rationalizing. At this point rationalization has effectively been thrown out of the window. Your ability think is affected by the way your emotions run wild. This can cause a distortion in your ability to think and affect the way you perceive the situation. Reminding your self that parenting is a marathon and not a sprint is the best way you can take control of the situation. These steps are necessary if you want to preserve the bond you have with your toddler, but also want to establish some boundaries or limits.

Chapter 5: Understanding Toddlers

What are the warning signs that your baby may have become a tot?

Your baby will begin to notice signs around twelve to 18 months. Your baby makes their first steps. These behaviors can be a sign they have reached the toddler stage.

What are some characteristics of this stage's design?

The baby has a new sense freedom and is now able unassisted to move more. Although the baby is eager to get out and explore the world, he or she remains very dependent on his parents. This can lead him to feel frustrated. The toddler sometimes acts erratically. While they may be able to make basic decisions, they lack the ability to fully comprehend them. They might choose two different things at once, and may get upset if they can't get them quickly. They don't know the difference. Any attempt to bargain with them, such as offering them choices, will usually be in vain.

The toddler is prone to acting on impulse and doesn't have the self control necessary for future planning. They are very focused on the present and can exhaust parents.

They do not yet understand that there is danger everywhere and that they need safety precautions. They can become wild and they are difficult to train. They are also very limited in their ability to remember what you say and do. You may need to repeat many times the instructions.

The toddler is not yet able to understand the impact of their actions on others. They are often reluctant to share their feelings or take turns, which can make socialization difficult.

They are also demanding a lot in terms of attention. Sometimes it can be hard to provide the necessary amount. The good news is that this phase is temporary and normal. This will help you recognize that your child is growing into a fun-loving, lively and excited person.

Common Discipline - Problems and Solutions

Each child is unique. But the challenges they face can vary. There are many common behaviors like bossiness, biting, and backtalking. Discipline is an ongoing learning process in which parents teach their children how they can make good choices. Positive parenting allows children to freely express themselves and learn how to behave properly, be considerate and respect rules. Positive reinforcement strategies and reactive strategies are necessary to help your child behave better. Discipline is not a good solution. Before you can correct misbehaviors you must understand why. Here are common issues parents face with disciplining their children, and strategies to overcome them.

Biting

Some children bite the person who feeds them. Other children sink their teeth in their siblings and playmates. Biting is a method of communication for children who don't have the language skills required to express their feelings. Biting is often an expression of frustration, not aggression or intention to harm.

Solution: Biting happens in childhood. Parents who respond with "ouch" or "that hurts!" quickly send the message to their child that biting should not be tolerated. You can communicate with your child by moving away from the biter and not attracting positive attention. It is important that a child who bites another child does not bite. Instead, say it clearly and make sure to tend to the victim, not the biter. Encourage the child who bites you to offer a hug and an apology.

If your child does routine biting, it is important to be alert for possible triggers. When a child displays frustration, help him to find the words to express it.

Hitting & Kicking

If a child feels frustrated, angry, sad, upset, or unable, they may strike or kick their parent or other playmate. As with other physical aggressions, a child who hits and kicks should not be labeled aggressive.

He needs to be taught how to express frustration.

Solution: It's similar to the reaction to biting. The strongest response is an "ouch!" followed quickly by "It doesn't okay to hit"/ "We don't hurt". This sends the message that physical aggressions are not acceptable communication methods. To stop the aggression, it's important to intervene immediately. Redirect the child to explain that, while it's acceptable to be upset it's not okay for the child to physically strike off. Encourage children's use of words to express their feelings, not their fists and feet. Teaching children to clap their hands when they're angry or feel the need to hit is a good way to teach them to do this. Never hit your child. This will send a clear message that hitting isn't okay. Children are more likely to hit if they see someone they trust.

Lying

Like adults, children make up the truth, as do many adults. Children lie when they feel threatened, insecure, or fearful of punishment or rejection. While the habitual lie can be concerning and can sometimes lead to low self-esteem, it's not uncommon for children to tell lies when they feel threatened or scared of punishment. Parents should dig deeper into the matter to find the truth.

Solution: Tell the truth when you're dealing with lying! There is always a reason for children to lie. Parents should find out the motivation behind your child's lies. To avoid disappointing parents, children often lie. Parents should evaluate their responses to their child's mistakes and ensure that the message is one of acceptance. Aside from being an honest parent (yes, this means that you should avoid even the smallest white lies), it is important to celebrate the truth with your child and teach the importance of telling truthful stories, even in difficult situations.

Factualizing (the merging between fantasy and reality) can be a normal part early childhood. Experts suggest that even if a child is telling a tall tale it's not a bad idea to have fun with him. Ask him what the stegosaurus he saw while playing at the park was and if he had a lot of fun visiting the volcano that erupted last nights when he thought he'd fallen asleep. A good imagination is often a sign of creativity and should not be discouraged.

Temper Tantrums

Young children can easily become frustrated when caught in a constant struggle between independence or dependence. These tearful eruptions not only exhaust and sometimes embarrass parents but can also be quite frightening for children as they lose control of their emotions without being able to regain control. A young child may quickly grow frustrated when she doesn't have the words to express herself.

Solution: While it's always good to try to prevent tantrums (staying consistent and realistic in expectations, avoiding excessive protectiveness, overindulgence, and staying consistent), helping a child manage a tantrum is the best strategy. While it can be hard for parents to control their child's tempers, it is possible to be a calm and steady presence during their outburst. It may be necessary to temporarily seperate the child from the chaos in order to help her regain some control. But, remain calm and kind. Instead of listening to a child's demands, which can be frustrating and time-consuming, help your child identify her emotions. Parents can encourage their children to use words like "You appear angry" or "Can you help rebuild that Lego Tower?"

Backtalking

Sometimes, it seems like a child is more capable of speaking than they are at actually talking. Children will quickly protest if they are told to do something they don't want to. "No" seems resonating throughout the household. Even though the opposition might be expected it's often what parents find most annoying.

Solution: It is better to address backtalk right away after it happens. She says that it is a gentle method of reminding and training children to give them another chance before they impose a consequence. Children often benefit from the opportunity to speak in a different way because backtalk is often just an honest, blunt reaction.

Interrupting

For children to be able to immediately share their urgent concerns and needs, they often just need someone to talk to. Children have a limited ability to understand the needs of others. This can lead them to feel less connected and valued.

Solution: While most parents' first reaction is frustration, a firm barked "Don't interrupt" is the best option. Before you talk to your child or make a visit with a friend, it is important to prepare them. Discuss with them how they can keep themselves busy while you're away. You could also suggest something or have them do it. It sends a clear message to your child that there is enough attention and time. Remind your child that announcements should not be made unless there is an immediate need. Additionally, teach your child how to recognize and respond to pauses in conversation so they can use an appropriate "excuse-me" phrase.

Bossiness

Many kids learn to get along with others. Some children want to lead, while others will follow. Even though parents are happy to have a natural leader in their children, it can be difficult for some little leaders not only to be demanding but also to become bossy and overbearing, which can cause even the most accommodating of playmates to leave.

Solution: Many times, it is simply a matter teaching children more cooperative ways of communicating. Children don't often realize the subtle distinction between assertive and respectful statements. Kids learn more easily when you suggest better ways to phrase things. Children learn better communication when their parents are patient and don't give orders.

Tattling

"She took me my doll!" Bailey says children struggle with setting boundaries with each other. Children don't have the skills or motivation to make decisions for themselves. Parents want their children to be able to resolve conflicts on their own. Parents can teach their children to manage conflict in a positive and effective way by teaching them to tattling.

Solution: The child may resort to tattling when she admits that she has no idea how to handle it. Ask the child what she thought of her treatment. This forces the child to look at her feelings and not at the actions of the other person. The parents should explain to the child what to say. For younger children, a simple "stop!" is a good place. For older kids, it's better to use the more elaborate "I don't want it when I take your toy." Children older than five years old need to wait their turn. Bailey says some children are naturally more assertive than the others. By helping children learn to define boundaries and resolve conflict, they become better able and more confident to make their own decisions and to settle future disputes.

Sibling Conflicts

Sibling fights will inevitable result from having more than one child. This can leave parents feeling like referees. Children want things to go their ways, and they get frustrated when they don't get what they want. It is not surprising that there will be conflict if you try to put three or four people who think the same way in the same room.

Solution: Parents may use sibling rivalries as teaching opportunities. Children do not have the capacity to resolve conflict on their terms. While you can support your child's right not to be angry, you can also help him avoid blaming his brother and suggest a better approach. It's sometimes a matter helping a child see his brother's point.

While it is normal for siblings to have conflict, rivalry doesn't have to be. Parent can ease jealousy by acknowledging the unique talents of each child and not comparing them. Sibling resentment can be minimized by encouraging cooperation, scheduling one-on one time with each child, as well as encouraging teamwork. Be present in those peaceful moments when your children play together. Children desire attention from their parents. It is a behavior that is strengthened and repeated that attracts attention. Do not intervene only in instances of disagreement, but also encourage cooperation and sharing among children. Accept and acknowledge both good and bad behavior.

Whining

It can happen anywhere: in the car, at home, at work, and most often when there are many other things to do (like getting out of bed, putting dinner on the table or getting everyone into the tub). Whining is typically a request for attention from children when they feel insignificant or ignored. However, it could also be a response either to hunger, fatigue, anger, or frustration.

Solution: Your child can calmly let you know that you won't listen to their whining. Also, that you do not understand whiny voices and that you will only respond to them when they stop whining. This is often a more effective way of dealing with your child. "Every time your children whine, you can take them on your lap and offer to give them a hug. This will help to prevent whininess by keeping children well-rested, fed, and ready to go. It's a great way to let your kids have fun and get them laughing with games like chase, playful tackle, or even a pillow fight. Markham says, "After fifteen minute of play, your child will be amazed at how cooperative he or she is for the rest" of the evening. What a sweeter feeling parenting makes you feel.

Parents can easily get discouraged if their children do not behave well. The problem is that parents often get discouraged when their kids behave badly. Being calm, confident, calm and consistent with your responses will go a long ways in teaching your kids how to control themselves. It will also help you get the day back to normal.

Chapter 6: Inside The Toddler Mind

If you've ever watched your baby's unblinking and solemn eyes, you know what parents have thought. A thrilling part of toddlerhood is getting to know your child's mind better and understanding how it works. This is where the most of your thoughts are revealed.

Here's an insight into the toddler's thinking processes. Why is she so passionate about everything? Your little discoverer is driven by curiosity. A toddler does not turn their curiosity on and of at will. She uses all her senses, including her eyes, to see and understand how things work. A 12-month-old child's curiosity is the reason she uses her hands and mouth to search for everything. She cannot help but be curious. At least the first instance, she is able to learn what's acceptable and unacceptable.

Is there a way he can tell time? A toddler can't use a calendar or a clock. Yesterday means any event that happened in the past. Tomorrow can be used for all purposes, but a child's conception of your time is not the same as an adult's. This is because they don't see themselves as adults until the second and third grade.

Your child exists in this and now for the majority of his or her life. The way your child marks time is through daily routines. Even a one-year-old can remember that there is breakfast, lunch, and dinner. If he's hungry, and sees you stirring the pans in your kitchen, he knows dinner will be at some point. However, he does not know how long "five minutes" or what "fifteen minutes" are. The pacing of the day is also helped by napping. Your child can feel reassured knowing that everything will be in order. It's like a relief from constantly checking your calendar or looking at your watch. This helps your child to understand the sequences of events and gives you a sense of control. We will continue vacation after the two remaining night-nights.

How many words does she remember? You'll be amazed at the amount she can remember. Even though many childhood memories fade away, toddlers can retain lots of details from their day. When you visit the bank, the bank teller will give your child a lollipops. You will see them recollect the steps of finger painting.

You can encourage your child's memory skills by asking questions, such as: "What was it like at the zoo?" Children often remember events that are unexpected and different from the norm. Instead of telling stories about the bears, lions, and tigers that surrounded them, your child might tell you about how he dropped his frozen dessert. A toddler may remember more about unusual events than what is written in the book, which could be an excursion to the zoo every year. Your child will be able to share his day at bedtime.

As your child grows in language skills, so does his ability to organize and save memories. Talking about trucks from a fortnight back to your child, or seeing seashells may bring back memories of vacations eight months prior, is a common sound. You can keep photos of distant relatives posted on the fridge and you can also look at family albums together.

How does his mind work Toddlers are known to be literal thinkers. They do not have an understanding of the subtleties that language, context and circumstances can create. When you say something like "You're funny", your child may counter, "I don't think so, Sammy!" Your child will start to develop abstract thinking at age 2. This includes the ability for your child to imagine things that aren't real. It is a way that children can learn that things exist even if they don't. This involves hiding objects and then returning them to where they were.

You can think of it as advanced peekaboo. If you look closely, you will see crackers beneath the couch cushions. Or blocks within a drawer. It helps a child build confidence and understand object permanence. Furthermore, it is a form of exercising control. Your child may be taking small control over a tiny portion of her universe by deciding what goes.

Does he have a good understanding of quantity? Your child's second year will help him understand basic quantities. A 1-year-old can grasp the concept of "more," "big," and "little" in a simple way. Your child could also be able, by age 2, to count to 2. A few bright 2-year-olds can easily recite the numbers 1-10. However, counting two or more is a skill that must be acquired by age three. For toddlers, counting songs such as "Ten Little Indians," are great fun and help them get familiar with numbers.

Does she know how to laugh? Your child won't be amused by irony or late-night comedians jokes. It's not easy to find humor in toddlers, but it's there. Slapstick may be a favorite pretending to subside, while your child can howl. Incongruity is another favorite. Toddlers find it hilarious if they call their nose "an elbow" or pretend to have a shoe. They also enjoy songs with silly lyrics and funny faces. Sometimes humor can be used to your advantage. You should always laugh with your child. Never at her. (At least not when she'll see you.)

What you can do

It's amazing to see the thoughts of toddlers while they play. This bear will fit in my pocket. What happens to the garments in my basket? How does it happen that the lights keep going on and off? This constant activity can seem as if it's play, mischief, big mess or just plain fun. However, to a toddler this is just a day's job--learning by doing. If you look closely, you will notice that he repeats the same task over and again. He studies cause, effect and, consequently, gravity as meticulously and as diligently as a researcher. Watching and copying what you do will help your child organize his world and learn how it works.

No one way toddlers can learn (or should) is through formal education. The idea of sitting down with a toddler to tell them "Now, let's learn how to read" or even "Let's learn colors" is absurd. It creates unnecessary pressure and makes it difficult to perform. Similar situations can be found in educational enrichment programs or other brainpower classes that are geared towards toddlers. It doesn't take fancy toys to help your child discover. Thomas Jefferson and Einstein didn't have them. Flashcards, by example, are great for toddlers to play with or shuffle through. You can make your child love these things if you talk about them every day: "Here are the yellow socks" or, "Here's a big and a little cup."

Spontaneous Learning preserves a child's joy about learning new concepts. All it takes is for you to answer your child's natural curiosity. And they will learn a lot.

Answering questions

Is it OK to ignore questions that are not relevant to my answer?

"What's that?" Could also be the number-one query in the second and third years of life. Toys and toddlers often ask confusing questions. It's important to answer them. A toddler does not want a long response to the question "Why don't boys have penises?" For example, you might prefer to say "That's why boys go to the urinal."

You won't be able to access an extensive explanation of reproduction.

"Why" questions escalate at age 2. Sometimes asking "Why" might be a child's way of keeping things going.

Step into your child's world. It's okay to just observe and listen to your child. Children learn best with their senses. For example, let your child enjoy eating pebbles as you walk. You might also be able to count the stars and smell the spices in your cupboard.

-- In normal speech, describe and compare. Your child may not initially understand all the adjectives, including big, cold heavy, sweet, purple, and sweet. But, use them. She's busy trying to sort and categorize everything around, and these words will help eventually, the nuances their meaning will become apparent, first for obvious words and then abstract ones (exciting). It's a slow, gradual process. You might not realize it, but a toddler does pick up more information this way than you may think.

To forgive your mistakes. Your child might move from blocks, books, and dolls to other toys. You may end up with a mountain of crayons and puzzle pieces. Refuse to make demands that your child move from one place to another. You'll find chaos in toddlers' lives because they're curious.

-- Read with your child. You don't need textbooks and first-grade primers. However, any age-appropriate text will give your child a chance to explore a whole new world. Books are an excellent way to begin conversations that teach. Books that emphasize concepts, such as colors or forms, can be paired with books that entertain, which are characterized by engaging stories, clever language, and beautiful illustrations.

Meltdowns

Toddlers lose it--a lot. A meltdown isn't like a temper tantrum. It's more of an extreme loss control that is usually triggered either by overwhelming feelings, frustration, or both. The day is full of difficult tasks (taking off a sweater to make the toy train move along the wooden tracks), and terrifying experiences (thunder, creaking doors). Your child does not have the communication skills necessary to convey his feelings, wishes, or needs. If you give your child too much, they may holler and cry, whine, shout, or even bite.

Be calm, but be kind. Instead of punishing or trying reason with a toddler meltdown, try finding a way to fix it. Sometimes, a distraction like dance or water play can be enough to soothe the crying toddler. The outdoors can be a great place to get away from the chaos. If your child gets upset about minor things, it could be time for a nap and a snack.

Make use of the opportunities for training that are available around you. Museums and symphonies provide wonderful educational experiences for older children. You can also find many interesting things right in your neighborhood for toddlers. The refrigerator is full of interesting shapes and colorful colors. The washer is loud and makes funny sounds. There's action everywhere, dirt everywhere, and large machinery. You won't be told to stay still or not run through the halls.

Use household objects to help toddlers learn

To discover the workings of the Earth, Toddlers do not need to use workbooks and fancy toys. You will likely already have the majority of those items in your drawers and cabinets.

Pots and saucepans
-- Measurement cups or spoons
Hand mirror (unbreakable).
-- Playing card m/ A ball made of string
Cardboard boxes (large, small and medium)
-- Rolling pin
-- 'Wooden clothpins
-- Laundry basket
-- Old magazines/catalogs
-- Aluminum pie tins
Wicker baskets
-- Keys on keychain
-- Adhesive tape
-- Dustpan und brush

Learning ways to be a better person

Basic manners is one kind of education that toddlers will be able to receive. The art of social introductions is not something toddlers are ready for. It is time for you to set the foundations that will enable your child to be polite, considerate and respectful.

Be kind to your self. It is easy to see that toddlers have very big eyes. Through their observation they pick up many lessons about behavior. Even though toddlers can be very self-centered, by following your example they will start to consider other people's feelings. They will be able to see you speak "Hello," "May we?" and "Excuse me." They will be able to see you saying "Hello,"" and "May it?"

Show your child how actions have an impact on others' feelings. Can you help your child feel better by thinking of how you can make it easier? This approach will help you to see the potential consequences of positive actions. "Does Aunt Sue's hug make you feel happy?" Let's hand a selection of the flowers to

Mrs. Smith, and see if that makes her smile.

-- Teach, please and many thanks. Your child will most likely consume many thanks. This is especially true if he hears that you say it every time he gives you something. For please, at first you will need to tell your child or prompt him: "Can't you say please?" Actually, your persistence will be rewarded and you'll continue prompting well into high school. But persistence will eventually pay off and the habit of prompting will become second nature.

Be able to recognize when it's time to let go. Be mindful of your child's developmental stage. An infant 18 months old may not be able understand the idea of sharing his toys with someone.

Toddlers & Computers

Ours is the first generation ever to be able to talk about computers with toddlers. It is an indicator of how deeply embedded computers are in our culture. Computer games as well as learning programs have the potential of amusing and benefiting children from preschool through highschool. So it is not difficult to bring the logic down. In any case, a one-year-old will imitate his mother banging the keys on the keyboard. A 2-yearold can operate a mouse. Even for the most tender years, software is abundant.

However, you should not be surprised if it concerns toddlers or computers. Although these programs are fun and engaging, they offer no academic start for a 1- or 2-year-old. Three-dimensional exploration, play and play are how toddlers learn best.

The interaction that a flat screen provides is very limited. It cannot be touched or mouthed. Through play. Some parents want to teach their children computers as young as possible. Computers will be so important in their lives. It doesn't matter how well-intentioned they may be, computer literacy is essential for today's toddlers. What computer knowledge they haven't been exposed too at 2 they will still consume lickety by 4 or 5.

Chapter 7: How to Stop Toddler Temper Tantrums

Temper tantrums among toddlers are not uncommon. Toddlers can have tantrums as they lack the communication skills and cognitive skills that toddlers need to express themselves. Toddlers also don't have the coping skill to deal effectively with negative emotions so throwing tantrums is often the most satisfying choice. There are many things that you can do to handle tantrums. There are many things you can do to stop tantrums. You can also teach your toddler healthy ways to express emotions.

Stop Your Toddler's Tantrum

Assess the situation. Before reacting, spend a few seconds to examine the source of your child's anger. Do you know why they are mad? Are they hurt or scared? How you deal will depend on why your child is upset.

Sometimes, it's best for the toddler to have their tantrums and not pay too much attention. This is especially true for children who are trying to manipulate you by throwing tantrums. If you feel that your child may be losing control, it is better to just let them go.

If your child is crying out of fear, or because they feel overwhelmed by a situation you should not ignore them. For them to feel safe, they will need your comfort.

It is not a good idea to try and reason with an angry toddler. In the midst of a meltdown, it is impossible to try and reason with a toddler. They are just too busy with their emotions to pay attention to what you say or hear. You may not understand their reaction, but remember that toddlers don't have the same reasoning skills and coping abilities as adults. They simply respond in a manner that makes sense for them.

However, this does not mean you should abandon your child and walk away if it is unsafe. You wouldn't want your child to sit on the ground in middle of busy grocery stores.

You can, however, let your child go wild in their room while you're away from home. Giving your child space is a great way for you to be able to express yourself without fighting.

Distract them. Distracting your child may be able to stop them from causing a panic attack. It may help to distract your child if they are already throwing a tantrum. It is best to choose something they're likely to like. Take a few items with you if you plan to travel to places where there is a chance of a tantrum.

If you feel that there is a danger of tantrums starting, pull out a piece of paper and say "Look what we have!" If they don't mind, hand it to the child. If they don't nod, then give it to them.

You can give the same advice if your child is throwing a tantrum. However it might prove difficult to get them to see what you are doing.

It's a good idea to have small toys and healthy snacks for distraction.

Do something silly. It is not difficult to get your toddler laughing. Make it silly for your child to distract from their anger. Laughter can also help to release chemicals in the brain, which will make your child feel better.

Try hiding behind something to make it seem like you're shopping. Then, smile big and start talking.

Don't give in. Do not give in when your child is having a meltdown. However, you shouldn't allow yourself to be frustrated or embarrassed into giving in. This is because it shows your child that they are capable of achieving their goals by giving in.

Try to get out of the situation immediately if you are embarrassed. If, for instance, you're at the grocery shop and your child starts screaming the moment you enter, you might think about putting off the shopping until later. It might be frustrating but it will be easier than dealing a cranky toddler through the entire shopping trip.

Keep your temper under control. Parenting is a hard job. You can sometimes just walk away, if necessary. If you feel as though you might lose your temper quickly, you should get out of the way. If your child is at your home, you can allow them to have a meltdown in a private area. Once they are done, you can go to another space where you can settle down for a few more minutes. If you are out, take your child along to the car. After they have settled in, you can go outside and take deep, calm breaths.

Many recommend deep, slow breathing while counting to ten to calm down.

If you feel the need to hurt your child, don't be angry. Call someone who can help. Contact your partner, friend or relative who can stay with your toddler for a few minutes. Parents will have to experience losing it at one time or the other. You can prepare for it and plan how you will deal.

Give your child positive attention to prevent future tantrums. If your child believes that throwing a tantrum is the only way to get your focus, they will likely use it as a way to get what you really want. If your child is behaving well, you should give attention. Do not hesitate to give your children lots of cuddles, love, and attention when you see them being happy. Don't give up on them if they are displaying negative behaviors.

For example, if your child does not throw a tantrum when you go to the shop, take them to a park to have a play or to pick out healthy treats. This will let them know that good behavior can have good consequences.

Limits and Punishments

Pick your battles. This is an important point to remember if you have a toddler. If you tell your child constantly that they can not do something, can have something or can touch it, they will start to feel like they have no control. This can lead to a lot of frustration and even a fight. Think about why you're saying "no", before you start to say "no", to any situation. If you aren't concerned about it, then allow them to have it.

It is possible to give your child more control by giving them more choices. As an example, you could let your child choose from several outfits. Allow them to choose one of the options at dinner. These are very small things that you won't notice, but will allow your toddler to feel like they have some control over their dinner.

Clear boundaries should be established for behavior. Your child's development is dependent on you setting clear boundaries. This does not mean you need to make your child feel like a dictator. It means you will show them that you respect their rights and are protecting them. Be mindful of why you're setting limits for your toddler. You might discover that some limits you set are unnecessary.

As important as safety limits are, so are respectable behavior and boundaries. It is important to set safety limits with empathy.

To illustrate, you could say to your child "When you cross the street with me, I expect that you hold my hand the whole way." You might find this boring. While you may want to have fun and run, there are cars on the street. You can get hurt by running into cars on the street. Let's go together and practice looking at cars.

Time out your child. Timeout is a well-known discipline method that can be used to punish a child's bad behavior. It is effective for many children. If your child is throwing fits, make sure they are in a safe place away from any toys or dangerous objects. You can give your child one warning. Explain what will happen to them if you don't comply. If they persist, take them aside and give them the time out. Turn on the alarm for the period of time you specified. For toddlers, the time out should be only for a few short minutes.

When time out is finished, ask your child whether they would like to talk with me. Do not force them to do anything.

Always give one warning. If your child is throwing a tantrum you can say, "If you don't stop this tantrum," and they will be placed in a timeout for two minutes. Keep warning them, but don't ignore the need to take action. It won't take long for the toddler to understand that you don't really mean your words.

Do not allow your child to be spanked. It is tempting to spank your child when your child is having a tantrum. Research shows that spanking is not a good way to reduce unruly behavior. But it can lead you to other serious problems that can last a lifetime. Children spanked by their parents are more likely have behavior problems or to suffer from mental illness.

Children spanked suffer from similar problems as those who are subject to "serious," physical abuses like punching or slapping. It is possible to spank your child in different situations, but it is still harmful.

You can give your child a firm hug if they are having a tantrum. It may be enough to soothe your child or end the tantrum.

Healthy alternatives for teaching your toddler

Try other ways for your child to communicate. Children as young as toddlers are still learning communication skills, so it can be difficult for them to communicate their needs. Parents have often taught their children signs to help them communicate what they want. You don't have to teach this to your children. There are other methods that you can use to try to understand what they're asking.

Ask your child to show what you want. If your child points in a direction, you can look at the point they're pointing to find out if you can follow their lead. If you are still having difficulty, let them point in the direction you were walking to see if it helps you.

Many parents also teach their children signs that indicate the items they frequently ask for. It can be water, food or milk.).

Sometimes it can help to place yourself in the shoes of others. How would you feel about if you needed or wanted something, but couldn't find the right solution?

Talk calmly with your child. It is only going to make things worse for your child if he or she senses you are angry. Instead of screaming or speaking in anger, try talking calmly with your child. Ask your child to share their needs with you by placing your hands on their shoulders.

Children are greatly affected by their surroundings. Being calm and collected will help children calm down quicker.

Be supportive of your child's emotions and don't make them feel bad. If you seek it out, temper tantrums can have a lot of value. A tantrum can be a great opportunity to teach your child how to behave when they're feeling bad emotions. Your child will experience many emotions during their entire life. While they may be more positive than negative, there will most likely be some. This is why you should not just tell your child that they are bad because they behaved that way. Instead of pointing out the bad behavior, suggest that they find other ways to express frustration.

You can, for instance, empathize if your child has thrown a tantrum after they couldn't find the toy at the store. As an example, you could say, "I understand why" to your child. It can be difficult when we don't achieve what we want. However, shouting and screaming won't help. Perhaps next time that you feel angry, instead of screaming at me, you can tell why.

Understanding why Tantrums are common Tantrums happen for one reason. A toddler might be throwing a tantrum when they aren't getting what they want or when something happens that they don't want. To vent frustration, a tantrum might be the result of a child not being able to communicate well. A tantrum is an attempt to control situations in which children can communicate.

This will keep you from seeing a tantrum or other signs that you are being insensitive. As a parent, you have the responsibility of knowing what is best for your child. So if your child is screaming at you because they aren't getting what you want, remind them that you are just looking out to their best interests.

Do not create a situation that is likely to fail. Unsatisfied children are likely to throw temper tantrums if they are bored, hungry or tired. This applies to both children and adults. It is easier to snap at your spouse if you are hungry or tired. Do not set a schedule that encourages your child to be unhappy.

If your child hasn't had lunch, or taken a break, they won't be able to plan a large shopping trip. When your child isn't getting what they want, it's almost certain that they will throw a tantrum.

It is important to understand that some children may be more sensitive than others. Children who are more sensitive will throw major tantrums. This is because sensitive children feel more strongly about their emotions and are more likely to throw major tantrums when they don't achieve what they want. However, your toddler can benefit from this sensitivity if you help them learn to express their emotions in a healthy way.

Keep in your mind that many of what your child does is to find out how the world works. They might throw a tantrum out frustration or anger to find out if they can get what they want.

Reach out to your doctor. To determine if your child is having more tantrums, intensely throwing them, or for longer times, contact your doctor. Talk to your doctor about healthy strategies to deal with tantrums. [16]

Although tantrums usually don't indicate something serious they may be caused by a child's learning disability or vision problems.

If you feel angry and unable to control yourself, it is a good idea to consult your doctor. Don't be ashamed. Instead, you should be proud of your ability to accept your limitations while also finding a way for yourself to better manage your emotions.

Chapter 8: An Reminder for Parents

Parents have the most demanding job in the whole world. To be able to discipline your child well, you must be in great shape. These simple reminders can help you remain consistent and not become too stressed.

Self-Control

Contrary the belief of most parents, it's not your toddler or his emotions that need to be controlled. But you have to take care of yourself. Parents must learn self-control. You won't manage your toddler if you don't.

Parents can make mistakes when they're angry. These mistakes include screaming at their child and spanking, or using demeaning terms. While meltdowns can be understood by adults as something you don't want, they are not meant for children.

He can become more self-conscious if he hears or does not like what you are saying. Be sure to keep your emotions on a normal level and, if you start to feel upset or are about to lose it, walk away.

Self-Timeout

The best way to stop yourself from saying or doing anything bad to your child is to have a timeout. You might not be the type of person who curses at or hits children, but stress situations can make you into one.

There will come a time when you just won't be able to understand your toddler. You will have difficulty sleeping and lose control. Do the following when you feel like you may be about to lose control.

Stop. Stop talking, stop negotiating or trying calm your son. Just stop.

Step away. Take your toddler to a safe space or location and go. Ask someone to substitute for you and get out of the situation.

Continue to take deep breaths for 3 minutes, then continue taking more. Keep taking deep, long breaths. Do this three to 10 more times. Or continue until your body is calm. Breathing is a great way to relax.

Recollect. Once you're able to calm down, it is time to take stock of the situation. Are you worried about your toddler being tired, hungry, or lacking sleep? Was he able to keep a promise you made but failed? Is he in pain or did you promise him something? Did someone take his toy, or is he just unable build with his blocks?

There are reasons that the situation doesn't seem too difficult. Once you're calm, you'll see that there isn't too much to it.

Know your Battles

Power struggles occur when a toddler and his parent feel their needs must be "followed" or win the argument. You'll have many power struggles with your child if you don't discipline them positively or consistently. Even then, your child will sometimes have intense needs that can't be satisfied by correct discipline.

During this time, it's best to just pick your battles and not get involved in power struggles. Sometimes, you just need to look at the situation objectively and assess whether it is worth the trouble. You don't always have to win when you're exhausted or in a hurry.

Take the time to teach your child how to behave. Reserve the right of raising the white banner for serious occasions like running late to a meeting or needing to rest after 36 hours work.

Chapter 9: Positive Discipline

For many generations, the quest for the best method to discipline children is a top priority of parents around the world. Perhaps child discipline is the most unpleasant aspect of parenthood for many parents. To instill discipline with toddlers can be difficult, exhausting.

Discipline, however, is not punishment. Discipline is not punishment. It is about teaching, guiding, informing and instructing children how to behave according the the community's standards. Discipline has no short-term goals. Instead, it is proactive and long-term.

Positive Discipline has become a very popular discipline method. It is based on a belief that all children are good. If they focus on their positive behavior, it will encourage them to demonstrate positive attitudes.

Positive Discipline: The Tactics

1. It is important to treat the cause rather than the symptoms.

It is not uncommon for a child to be disruptive or act out in a way that isn't right. If a child starts crying, throwing tantrums, hitting his sibling, or screaming out loud, there is a reason. Sometimes, the child is just trying to get your full attention.

Positive discipline allows you to see the whole picture and understand that your child is experiencing a need. He is using tantrums to express his feelings. Understanding the root cause of an action or behavior will allow you to solve it permanently.

2. You can tackle misbehavior by using logic and empathy

Empathy refers to the ability of understanding and relating to others' emotions. Empathy allows you to get in touch with your emotional level. It can be empowering and healing. In parenting terms, logic allows children to make sensible decisions, make mistakes, and experience logical/natural results.

Jim Fay's Love and Logic embodies these principles. It's a philosophy that suggests dealing with the child's misdemeanors with empathy and not punishment. It helps parents make parenting more rewarding and enjoyable by using loving, calm solutions and building genuine connections. Your child may throw his toy at a wall. Do not react immediately by screaming. Instead, you can manage your reaction by being calm and controlled. Your response can be even sung. This signaling to the child to cease is effective in disarming tension and encouraging cooperation.

* "Uh-oh! It was said that your car toy is being thrown again.

3. If the child seeks attention, you should show them productive ways of interacting with it.

Toddlers want a lot from their parents and will often seek out help to achieve their goals. Your attention can give your child emotional security as well as affirmation that you care about him. Your child might be seeking connection if he acts out often despite his basic needs being met. It is possible to give your child tasks and teach him positive ways of using his energy. This will teach your child how to use their energy constructively rather than throwing tantrums and acting out.

* "Please tie you shoelaces."

4. Instead of saying "No", redirect your child's eyes.

When their toddlers behave badly, parents often say "No," or "Don't," Younger children tend to mimic their parents, seeing this as a fun game. Many children disregard the commands of their parents because they point out what they cannot do.

Positive discipline is about focusing your attention on the solution and showing your kids what they can do. One strategy to help your child focus his attention on something positive and exciting is to do so. Redirecting his attention to positive activities instead of misbehavior is another important strategy.

To illustrate, if your child begins to be bored or annoyed in the grocery, you can immediately distract his attention by asking him for the things he wants and placing them in the shopping basket.

* "Can you place this item in our grocery shopping cart?"

5. Dole out your "energy consequences."

It is also known under the "energy drain principle" as a way to regain your energy. It is similar to picking your victories and diffusing tantrums.

* "It really upsets us seeing you with this type of behavior. It seems like I won't have the energy or the will to play with your this afternoon in a park.

6. Respect your boundaries

Setting reasonable, attainable, specific and loving boundaries is a way to help your child feel safe and responsible. Examples include being honest, being kind, or being respectful.

Always explain the reason behind the rules and provide examples of what you expect him to do. Young children love to bite, hit and grab toys from others. Tell your child what the consequences are. This helps him understand the consequences of his behaviour and how to avoid it.

* "If I bite or hit my playmate, it hurts him. He will not play anymore with me."

7. Giving him a spokesman.

If you pay attention to your child and listen attentively when he speaks, you can demonstrate how special your child is to you. It makes him feel valued and loved.

Here are some tips for giving your child a voice.

It is okay to stop what you are doing. Instead, look into his eyes. You can also create a regular time for "talk", at least 15 minute per day.

* Let him speak for his self. When possible, let your child speak his mind and express his emotions. Do not criticize. Let him speak out about his problems and concerns. You can then help him identify solutions to his problems by asking him about other options.

Respect his opinions. Never end his sentence. Let him share his thoughts and emotions. Allow him to feel free and have the time to tell you what troubles him.

Encourage him as an expert in something. When you recognize and name him an expert (e.g. Music Expert or Name Expert), it boosts his confidence to express their knowledge, wisdom and skills.

* If the child confesses to something or shares a troubling experience, it is important that you stop reacting. You could say "I'm grateful that you told me this." You did the right things by informing me.

What's next?

You must remain calm and calm in order to not cause an upset. He will lose his trust and close your eyes to you. To keep his trust, you must remain the first person he calls when he is in a critical situation. You must listen with your whole heart, mind, ears, eyes, mouth, and soul. Doing so will create a lasting impression on your son's self-worth and remind him that he is valued.

8. You don't have to feel embarrassed about making mistakes.

Shame is powerful. It can cause a change in the child's attitude and ego. It does not leave a mark on the child, but it can make him feel bad about his self-worth. If not well processed, it can bring about the following consequences:

* It impairs his ability to internalize values, and to learn from the mistakes he makes.
* It makes him compliant and ineligible to avoid future shame, which reduces his ability make better choices.

It makes him think he is a naughty, poor boy, disappointed or a failure. He doesn't understand that his behavior does not define him.

* It makes him focus on his flaws, failing to understand empathy which is essential for healthy relationships with others.
* It makes the child judge, righteous, critical or judgmental when others make mistakes.
* It makes the children feel helpless, powerless and insignificant. It causes him to seek out people who can be vulnerable and more easily defended.
* It encourages secrecy to preserve his integrity. If truth is revealed to him, he will seek to cover it up.
* The child may believe it is acceptable to be judgmental, righteous or critical of

others' mistakes. These are all ways of dealing with problems that are harmful.

* It makes him not accountable for his behavior, encouraging denial about ownership.

One aspect of positive discipline is to encourage families and friends to talk about their mistakes. Dr. Jane Nelsen suggests that children learn to accept mistakes as learning opportunities by encouraging everyone in the family to share a mistake they made or learned from during the day.

The ways to eliminate shame

* Don't make fun of the child's feelings or actions. This will make him feel less than he should be.

"You want to have more? You already have many toys but still want more. Don't these toys suffice for you?

"Are you a baby? Can't yo see that i am busy taking good care of my little brother?"

"If your skull is not securely anchored in your body you will lose it!"

* Don't criticize or judge.

"Does that big car toy appeal to you? We won't be buying toys for you today, darling. If you still love it, we will buy the toy on your birthday.

"Sweetheart. I will always love you, but I am unable to carry you now. You can give me a bear hug."

* Encourage your child's positive behavior by modeling them. Young children often look up to their parents, mimicking what they do. Use this to influence your son by doing what you tell him. Be patient, kind, and tolerant while maintaining your boundaries.

* Do not guilt-trip by bringing up past mistakes.

* Don't label your child as the "funny guy". It can embarrass your child if some of his friends or family make fun of him, or call him "not very funny", when he does not display "funny" antics.

* Concentrate on behavior only

You shouldn't make any comments about who he really is. Hitting is not an appropriate way to express your anger.

* Talk about your feelings regularly with your child to increase his emotional literacy. Teaching the child that it is OK to be upset, frustrated, or angry. But, he must have control over his emotions and not allow himself to get carried away by them.

Treat your child as the person you want. As a parent, the power and influence you have to help your child become emotionally responsible, strong, competent, capable, beautiful, and independent. Instill this positive image of your child by telling them "I am a loving parent and won't intentionally hurt anyone. So what are you going to do?" By allowing him to see through his behavior, you are encouraging him to feel empowered.

* Do not compare the child to any other children, including his siblings. This will make him feel ashamed and insecure if he doesn't measure up to them. Under your supervision, allow him to explore his interests. Encourage him and not force him to take up different paths of learning.

* Use the antidotes to shame, courage and vulnerability. Recognize that the child can be frustrated, guilt-ridden, or sad. Encourage him to show that he is kind, strong, brave, and capable of handling many situations. "I get that you are upset about not getting a top grade in Math. It's fine to feel frustrated. However, you can improve the next time. Just find the best way to do it.

9. Prioritize quality time.

It will make your child feel special and give you a sense of belonging by spending quality time together. Children are hungry for attention and the best way is to create regular bonding times. It helps to make it a priority. This makes the child feel more secure, happy, settled, and capable in overcoming fears and frustrations. Also, it is a magical experience to spend time with your child as you enter into his world.

It makes you more compassionate. It helps you to be sensitive to your child and understand his feelings. Your child can draw from you the necessary skills and learnings that will shape his future and help him reach his full potential. This deeper bond creates a sense of connection that is calming and loving, which helps you cope with the fast pace of living in a hectic world.

It reminds us of the beauty and innocence of childhood. Spending regular time in the company of your child will bring back many childhood memories. You also get a new perspective on life, and you are reminded of the beauty and goodness that surrounds us.

It transforms the bond. Your attention encourages the child's fears, doubts, or feelings. He will feel more confident in expressing himself in your presence, and he will be excited to discover what you have planned together. Your time and your complete presence are two of his greatest gifts.

It helps heal deep wounds. Perhaps your child is carrying deep hurts, fears or worries that aren't obvious to you. He may be afraid to share these feelings. Your child will be more open to sharing his deepest feelings once you have built trust, empathy, and deeper emotional connections. When your child is sure that you will listen and understand him, it will be easier for him to share his vulnerabilities. It will also help him to talk about his experiences which will ultimately lead in healing and catharsis.

It can open up profound feelings and provide insight. Being able to spend quality family time is an amazing experience for a child. It releases his uncertainty and insecurity. It generates a lot of love, joys, understandings, and deeper insights on the important things in your life.

It is a source of balance and empowerment. The quality of your time with your child will allow you to be a better parent. Perhaps you are looking for ways that to build a better relationship with your child. Or how to get rid off childhood traumas. This is a time to let go past traumas and embrace new beginnings. Allow yourself to be fully immersed in the child's world and you can heal childhood traumas.

It encourages communication. A happy family will be built on healthy communication. You can make your child feel more at ease talking about his secrets if you make the effort to spend time with him.

It develops positive behavior. Children who spend more time with their parents develop a greater sense of responsibility and are more willing to behave well. Toddlers learn by watching their parents. Set aside some quality time to show your toddler how amazing you are. This will encourage him to emulate what you do and to pass on the knowledge to his peers.

10. Don't be the control freak, but be the leader.

Do you prefer to be a leader or a boss? You must define your role as parent. What you do and how your do it can have an impact on the development of your children.

As a leader you will become more aware that you have vital responsibilities to raise responsible children. You're able to discipline your child and enforce your parenting methods. Your role is important and you should not lose sight of it. Begin your personal journey as a parent by raising a child.

You can become a boss parent if you don't define your job. You are often affected by moods and other small stimuli that can be arbitrary. To control a child, he or she may use command phrases like "Go brush the teeth now!"

The parent who leads might ask the child, "How do your teeth stay clean and healthy?". While the controlling model of parenting encourages resistance, the leader makes it feel like the child is valued and that in turn stimulates his cooperation. Leaders make it easier for children to succeed by allowing them to have control of the situation and allowing them the freedom to choose. In order to get their children's compliance, controlling parents use fear and anger. However, children who are forced to obey because of intimidation can often act defiantly and aggressively.

What makes a leader and parent a better parent?

1. Your needs come first. You give priority to your child's welfare over your own.

2. The tone you set is important. Your role is to create an environment conducive for child comfort and protection. Even if you feel under pressure or have to deal with difficulties, it is important that you maintain a caring and positive attitude while taking care your child.

3. You become extremely adaptable. It is not easy to have a toddler. At one point, they are happy, at the other, they are screaming and screaming. Good leaders should be ready to change strategies when the current one doesn't work.

4. Celebrate small milestones. Recognize and praise your child for his achievements and failures. Children love tangible rewards and positive reinforcement. So be generous in your encouragement and praises.

5. Do it with love It is pure love to experience parenthood. It is not easy, but it will bring you great joy and inspire you

to be a better leader. You must dig deeper to create a stronger emotional attachment with your child and connect with him more often to ensure his success.

The leader-parents can also use these other methods:

* Less modeling and more ordering
* Listening that is more active and engaged, rather than less assumed
* Do not jump into conclusions
* Before you enforce the consequences, it is important to empathize and understand the reasons behind the behavior.
* Encourage your child to succeed but also allow him to make errors
* Prioritizing connection, and building relationships

Respecting the child's right to attention, affection, comfort, and desire to be independent, make choices, have space, and take control of their time.

* Avoid imposing preferences on your child and allowing him to make his own decisions
* To promote kindness, generosity, compassion, and respect

* Modeling good behaviors
* Moving away from raising compliant children and towards raising intelligent, respectful, responsible, happy children
* Coaching positive behavior and not asking/dictating children to display certain behaviors
* Don't use "because i said so" or the "because i am your mother!" phrases. They should be used in a deliberate manner.

Chapter 10: Develop cooperation, responsibility and affection

If you give your toddler the very best care and love, it will help him become well-adjusted. Because your toddler knows that you are there for him, it is vital that he trusts you. The trust you build with your toddler in his early years will make him feel more secure and less anxious. He will trust you to make laws and limits, and he'll realize how much you love him.

Real life example: Your 12-months-old son or daughter may love playing with you, but might get annoyed or upset when you are asked to leave. It is vital to teach your baby that it is okay to be angry or upset. You must manage toddler frustrations, as well as your emotions. By doing this, your toddler will learn how to trust you. There will be lots of fun games later.

Consistent

It is crucial to be consistent in disciplining children. When parents fail to follow the rules and consequences established for their child, it is often difficult to train them. For example, if your child is exhibiting bad behavior and you say that timeout is the consequence, you must follow this instruction. Your power will be diminished by empty threats. Keep in mind that children learn from their parents to be watchful. It is important to be a role example. If your child asks you to gather toys, it will be much easier for you to feel satisfied if you have put them away instead of rummaging around.

Fight With Anger

Babies between 2 and 3 years old often have great feelings of anger, frustration, and hostility. Their social and emotionally-skills are just starting to improve. You can help your toddler do well by listening to them, adapting to the environment, distracting from it, and preparing to face difficult circumstances.

Remain calm

If your toddler attempts or attempts to reach for dangerous or inappropriate objects, be calm and say "No" to stop them from running. You shouldn't hit or spank your child. It is highly unlikely that children will begin to associate actions with punishment. The message you send when you spank people is that it's OK to hit someone when you're mad. Researchers say spanking is no different to other techniques like timeouts.

Speak the Language of Your Kid

Avoid contacting your child if you are upset. Your child will understand when you are talking to him. The simple act of saying to your child "I can understand why you are upset" will show him you are trying to understand and expand his emotional vocabulary.

Example: A friend gives you a toy car. Instead of giving it a timeout, or trying to justify why it was wrong, give the toy instead to the other child. Try to eco-echo what your child is thinking and feeling back to him. "I know that you want the truck." This will help your child relax if you can validate his feelings. Remind him to keep it simple: "No grabs, no grabs, this is max's turn." It may initially feel ridiculous, but it's going be a success!

To Avoid, Don't Use the "No" Word

Many toddlers start to use "No" in their first sentences. This is almost always the one they use the most. This is important for parents. Your child will not repeat the "No" phrase over and over again.

An example in real life is: You served lunch to your baby, but he did not eat the banana you brought him. Ask him/her if the banana is something they would like to eat. However, you can still give the banana later. However, your baby will be able to understand that the word "No", even if it is resisted by you, can have some weight. Even though the banana will be taken away, your toddler may realize that something isn't right and stop saying it.

Restore and Replace

Young children learn from doing. It's okay to let your child do something you don't agree with. It's not your job to support your child when he or she reaches out for dangerous things. Give the object back or make your child push you. You can then offer him a healthier alternative. It's important to explain everything to them, even though they may not understand. They will learn that such behavior is unacceptable. Exemplary of real-life: Your 12-month old finds your necklace box and has fun with it. Because it's colourful, your toddler loves it. You even saw him wearing your necklace. Instead of letting him keep the necklace, you can remove it and state that your jewelry box does not constitute a toy. Your child can now play with colorful toys by giving it to you.

Take corrective action

Your toddler will learn how to press the buttons and pay attention at some point. This is usually around the second birthday. It is important to distinguish between throwing peas on the ground when they are investigating their food from throwing them there in an intentional response. You can tell when he is looking at you and dropping his meal. It's his way of showing him that his actions have consequences. Exemplary of real life. A toddler made a mess beneath his highchair. After he's finished feeding, pick up the chair, place it on a flat surface, and ask him for help with his peas. Tell him, "Look, the floor looks messy, because I dropped peas. So you need to clean that up."

Responsibility Lessons and Toolbox

You can be a role example and parent to your child. There are many things that you can do for them to make their lives easier, such teaching responsibility by your actions.

A responsibility map is one of best selling products. There are many options and they are ideal for anyone over two. The charts not only keep track and remind you of good behavior, but also help you manage your household. Many of these charts are magnetic so that you can easily change the information. It is possible to list your child's behaviors and emotions as a way for them to see how you are behaving.

You may think it's too much for your child to handle, or even point out the good and the bad. Rewarding the right behavior is not enough. Sometimes a child may receive one sticker, while other days they might have received two. Just like the stickers on the hand, the key is showing your kids how proud you feel about them.

One guard tried something like that. The deal was that a jar with marbles would then be used. A marble would be added to the jar for every display of "please, Thank you", and other fine behaviors. The act of helping a toddler was a way for parents to express their pride in their children's abilities to be kind, respectful, curious and well-behaved. This was also a way for the child to earn "chore" funds. It was a way for children to earn some extra money by being responsible and respectful at the end.

No matter how you organize your toolbox, the key is to focus on the positive and not the less. Don't shame your child. But, show pride in your child by demonstrating your appreciation and showing love for their good behaviour.

It's up for you to decide if the chart, jar, and check marks are what you prefer. It should be tangible enough that your child can see it all day.

Your words and actions should reflect your responsibility. If you can say, "I'm sorry. This is the last thing I want to do, but if it takes ten more minutes, I'll play," this is better than giving in and ignoring your responsibilities. Although it can be frustrating to focus on your tot and work on time, your toddler will not learn if you do not show them responsibility.

There are many different ways that you can both teach responsibility and show affection. Below are some examples.

You work remotely. Your toddler may want to play but it is "parent' time. Your toddler should play with their toys or on their own. You can repeat the request from your child. Use their words and be respectful. In short, these phrases represent responsibility, ending soon and playing. You can set a timer for your breaks. Set up an activity for your child. Maybe you need your papers sorted or you accidentally left out some paper clips. You can teach your tot how to put them away. It is important that they are able to participate in the activity. So they are helping you, but not hindering your ability to focus on them.

You work from your home. You have an eight hour job during the day. Also, you have to prepare dinner, take care of your children and meet their needs. It is important to show love, respect and affection every day. Your toddler needs to be included in the routine. Let's imagine that you leave for work at 4:00 pm and that dinner is at 5:30 pm. After you arrive home at 5 pm, give your child hugs and kisses. Then, take a moment to talk about your day. Next, invite them to help you with dinner. Interacting, giving affection, and making sure you show responsibility, as well as offering what they have missed. After dinner, it's time to have some fun. Playing with your child after dinner can help you avoid a lot of yellow-light behaviors. Enjoy time playing, learning numbers, alphabets, or simply having fun with your child. When the "playtime" is over, which you may have established early in the routine, you can return to your responsibilities (including the dishes). If your child would like to help, then let them. If your child is not interested in helping, they can find something else to do while you complete the task.

Chapter 11: What Are the Stress Factors For Children?

Many parents and caregivers believe that their children are happy and carefree in the world. It is clear that kids don't do any things that cause stress like pay bills or keep a job. This creates the illusion that kids don't have stress.

It is important to remember that children have the same worries as adults and can feel stressed. They do, in fact, experience it a lot.

Stress is when we try to meet all of the demands. Most of these external demands come from family, friends or jobs. You may also find your stress sources within yourself. This is often when conflict arises from the difference between what we're capable of doing and what we do.

Anyone can feel stress as long they feel overwhelmed. Children can experience anxiety from divorce. The stress that older kids feel can be caused by peer pressures (mostly trying to fit into) or academic demands.

Sometimes, your child is too busy to do creative things after school or have time for relaxation. Overscheduled children might complain about everything or refuse to go to activities. Begin a discussion with your children about how their extracurricular activities are affected by what's going on in the family. If they complain you should explain the benefits and disadvantages to quitting an activity. If that is the case, you should work with them to figure out how they can manage their own time so that anxiety can be reduced.

The stress of your kid can go beyond what is happening in the home. Do you ever let your children hear you talk about problems at work, home, family, or even arguing with your spouse before your kids? Talking about these issues should be handled with care and not in the presence your children. This is because they can pick up on you anxieties and can become anxious.

Images like those depicting wars, terror and discussions about natural disasters can cause children to be concerned about their safety as well as the safety of the ones they love. It is crucial that you monitor what your children watch and listen to on TV. This will help you decide when to explain it to them.

Make sure to mention any complications like divorce, death of a close friend or chronic illness to your kids. If they do not understand these messages, it may cause them to be more stressed and worry. Even the most amicable separation can be extremely stressful for children. They are experiencing major changes to their family's basic security system. Parents should not leave their children in a state they cannot choose, as this could lead to them being subject to criticisms from family members.

A normal adult's stress level might not be the same for a child. It is important to let your kids know that it is okay to feel upset.

Signs and Symptoms to Help Your Child

Get Stressed

It can be hard to observe if your child is stressed. The good news is that parents can help their child recognize signs of stress by observing changes in behavior, such as mood swings or acting out. The physical symptoms of stomachaches and headaches have also been noted in children. Take note of any signs your child may exhibit such as a withdrawal and inability to spend time with others, and when they are distracted or unable work on homework.

Children younger than 5 years old may have an unusual habit such as thumb sucking, finger picking, or hair twisting. Defiance of authority, lying, bullying and other signs that they are stressed could be indicators for older children.

It could indicate that your child is stressed by not wanting to be left or having nightmares or hyperreacting to minor incidents.

How to reduce stress with your kids

It is crucial to help your child deal with stress. There are several ways you can help them. The best ways to help your child cope are good rest and healthy nutrition.

Spending time with your child is a great way to help them. Although you don't need to talk the whole time, it will help your child see that you will always have their back. Children will trust you enough in their ability to help them and be open with you about anything that is going on. It's easy for them to trust you when they spend time with you on fun activities.

You don't have to be with your children anymore just because they are older. While it may be more difficult to stay home due to your work schedule, you still have the time to speak with them. Your interest will let them know that you care about them.

Your kids will feel more comfortable talking with you about what is causing stress. You need to offer solutions. Both of your minds can be gathered and you will come up with some solutions. They are more likely to stick with the plan if they know that they were part in the planning process. It could mean cutting back on after school activities, spending more with family, creating an exercise program, or keeping a journal.

We will also discuss how you can help your kids cope with stress. Knowing the top causes of stress for kids can help protect them.

If your child is going to have a doctor's visit to relieve stress, it's important to let your older siblings know. You might not need to prepare your younger children for a doctor's appointment, but it is important that they are aware of the details and how appropriate it will be for their age.

Also, it is okay for your children to feel stressed from time to time. Let them know it's normal to feel upset, scared, lonely, anxious and sad from time-to-time. It is important to let them know that they can manage these feelings.

Noticing when a child is stressed

Children react differently to stress than adults. It is because stress can cause panic in children. It all depends on the way their parents help or teach them to handle stress. How trusting their parents are with them will also affect how they reach out for support.

You may not have a close relationship but your child will want you to help them. We have some tips for parents who suspect that their child is suffering from stress.

It is important to notice the difference. If you notice that something isn't right about your child, tell him. Let them know that something is bothering your kid. If you're able to, let them know what you think is bothering them. Do not make it sound accusatory. This will help your children build up defenses for their own self-defense. Make it casual, and let them know that you are listening if it is something they are comfortable discussing. They should feel understood and that you are there for them if they need.

Listen to what your child has to say. Listen to what your child has to say. Your body language should reflect interest, patience. Openness, compassion, and empathy. Avoid judging, blaming, lecturing, or pointing out what they should have done. Your child should be able to express their concerns. They should also know that they can talk whenever they like. Without hurrying them, take your time to hear their entire story. They should be listened to carefully.

You can briefly comment on the feelings of your child. For example, you might say "Wow, that must be upsetting for you." or "I now realize why you were sad that they wouldn't let me into the game." This will help your child feel that you have listened and are understanding. Children feel better when they know that they are being listened to and understood. It also makes you seem more supportive, something they need to feel calm and at ease when they are stressed.

Give it some label. It's possible that younger children won't be able to articulate what they feel. It is important that your child knows what to do if they feel depressed or confused. You can help your children communicate better and increase their emotional awareness by using words. This is the ability of recognizing their emotional state. An emotional boiling level is when your children display emotions through their behavior, instead of communicating with words. Giving them a label helps them to not get to that point.

Talk to them about what they should do. If you both know the source of their stress, you should discuss the solution together. Encourage your child to participate in the brainstorming process and to come up with their own solutions. While brainstorming ideas, keep in mind that you do not have to do the majority of the work. Your child's participation builds confidence. Let them know that you support and encourage their ideas. Ask them how they believe their ideas will go. This will enable you to gain a better understanding of what is going on inside their heads.

Listen and you can move on. Sometimes your child just needs you to listen. These moments should be easy to spot. They will find that soon after doing this, all their frustrations will disappear. Once you have noticed that they have done this you should move on to a topic that is more positive and relaxed. You can help your child find something that will make you feel better.

Chapter 12: Food Fight

If we took a poll of parents with toddlers to ask them about their children's eating habits, it is not surprising that they would complain about their toddlers' appetite fluctuations, picky eating habits, or poor table manners.

It may be helpful to start by shifting our perceptions about how our toddler eats. Parents and caregivers can use these early years to build a healthy relationship between food and their toddlers. Power struggles and pressure can cause anxiety about eating and make it difficult to choose the right food. This can also lead to future picky eaters.

A healthy relationship to food is one in that food is being used for nutrition and health, not for comfort or the appeasement of others. If we create a situation in which toddlers have to eat a certain quantity of food to appease us or follow an arbitrary rule, we are teaching them that their relationship with food should be externally driven and not an intuitive one in which food is consumed for their nourishment.

This is one of those spots that can prove to be particularly difficult for parents and caregivers. All parents know that toddlers should eat. How come toddlers sometimes seem to be content just with a handful cheerios? This is normal. These toddler appetites can fluctuate greatly from day one to day and even at meals. This can be due to the fact that their bodies are experiencing growth spurts. A new and exciting world is available to them every day, making it easy to choose to play rather than to eat.

The Academy of Nutrition and Dietetics recommends the division of responsible in feeding. Ellen Satter (a family therapist, nutritionist and dietician) developed the division-of-responsibility in feeding model or DOR. The success of her model for encouraging and guiding children to a healthy relationship about food has been demonstrated time and again.

DOR model's ultimate goal, according to Ellen Satter Institute, is to promote what they call eating competency. This refers to healthy food relationships. DOR gives parents and caregivers guidelines to follow starting in infancy when it comes to feeding children.

DOR guidelines say that toddlers' food choices, including when and where it is offered, fall on their parents. However, toddlers decide how much they will eat. This may sound strange, but it is important to understand that caregivers as well as parents have to ensure that their children are given healthy, nutritious food. It is also crucial that parents trust that their kids will eat what they are offered. It takes trust that our toddlers don't starve, and structuring mealtimes in a way that allows toddlers be active participants instead of passive bystanders who are being fed.

There are many options to encourage toddlers to be active participants at mealtimes and allow them to take responsibility for their own meals. One way is to ensure that your toddler eats at least one thing on their plate. Perhaps your toddler loves apple slices and is currently on an apple binge. Your toddler might like slices of white cheddar cheese or rotisserie chicken. But, it's okay to offer a lunchtime menu that includes a variety of foods. Make sure there are some apples included so that they can enjoy the food. This is a way to set up both caregivers as well as toddlers for success.

Toddlers don't like being at odds with parents and caregivers. They do not like being in situations where they make their parents and caregivers feel annoyed or get into trouble. They don't wish to be made to eat food they don't enjoy or that they are not in the mood. This is like an adult that doesn't feel hungry one day but chooses to snack on granola bars instead of eating a full meal. This is the idea behind allowing our toddlers an opportunity to learn about their bodies and develop a healthy relationship with food. What number of adults had to finish every meal before they could leave the table as children? What was the point?

The economic aspect of not wasting food is important, but so is the message to the body and mind. Eating is not something you do for nourishment. It's a mindless task, which must be completed until a predetermined amount is consumed. This is not a healthy relationship to food. We see it in our culture through people who have conflicted values regarding food like comfort eating, binging, and calorie restriction.

There are additional ways to set parents, caregivers and toddlers up for success during mealtimes. Participate as much as possible with your toddler in the experience. You could ask your toddler for the color they want their water in. What color napkin are you using? What color is your plate? Ask your toddler to set up the table with their napkin, utensils and fork. You can give your toddler options such as "Would like to have 3 or more apple slices?" Is yellow cheese preferred or white cheese? Your toddler should be allowed to make these choices. If you aren't able or willing to honor it, don't give your child the option of choosing between different cheeses. If the dishwasher has the red and green cups, then you shouldn't offer either one.

Giving toddlers the freedom to make their own choices about their experiences is a way to give them a sense and autonomy. It also increases toddlers' involvement in the mealtime experience. It is also possible to let your toddler eat what they want. Provide proper utensils. Make sure your toddler is familiar with how they work. Show your toddler how to use them. Allow your toddler to use their fingers for picking up avocado cubes. If they are interested, you can let your toddler pick up each spaghetti noodle one at a while to help further develop their fine motor skills. You must remember that meals are still an important part of their explorations and learning. They are learning colors, textures and taste. It is this control that many of the negative emotions and associations that toddlers, their caregivers, and parents have about food, mealtimes, and meals, can be attached to. The caregivers and parents control the how, when, where and how often they feed their toddlers. However, they have no control over what the toddler eats or if any of it is eaten at all. This is an important part to helping your toddler develop a healthy relationship with food.

The environment you create for your toddler to enjoy food is an important factor in their healthy relationship. A table should be set up where family can have conversations and enjoy their meals together. This small step is important because it will impact how much time a toddler is able spend at a table where there are family members who are talking to and interacting with each other. The first example is showing that mealtimes should be comfortable and enjoyable. The latter shows that mealtimes don't have to be boring and should be enjoyed. A toddler's inability to stay still at a long table with their family is something that must be acknowledged. You can let go of this expectation and realize that your toddler may have stopped eating their food and are now trying to get down. This is their way of letting you know they cannot sit still for long periods of time. Communication is key to toddler behavior. This is what a fussy, wiggly toddler telling their parents or caregivers.

Helping a picky eater

The opposite effect of this is to bribe, negotiate, and use threats during meal time. Children who feel pressured or coerced will be less likely to cooperate. If your child has a fussy eating disorder, it is important to be realistic.

Here are some strategies that can be used to reduce conflict at mealtimes:

Encourage independence. Let your child help prepare meals. They can transfer food items with their hands from one bowl into another. After they're successful, they can learn more advanced skills like mashing and kneading. Allow your child to help put their own food on the plate. Allowing your child to take charge of mealtime will decrease the need for fights.

Provide variety: Your child should be offered a wide selection of healthy options. Children are more likely to eat a wider variety of foods, even if the portions are smaller. If your child refuses to eat certain foods, don't force them to. But, continue to make it available.

You can help your child eat healthy by focusing on good eating behavior. Show your child how you would eat and behave when you are with them at dinner. Show your child the things you love and how you eat them. Show your child that you can eat a wide variety of foods without being negative.

Chapter 13: The Healing Power of Tantrums

What is a Tantrum exactly?

Temper tantrums can cause frustration. It's a fact. They are not a problem, but they can also be an educational experience for everyone. If your child isn't taught better, he or she will throw tantrums. These can happen when your child is experiencing extreme emotions and is uncertain about how to manage them. With that in mind, it is important to approach tantrums calmly and with understanding.

Tantrums could range from screaming, hitting, or even holding one's breath. Some children, especially stubborn ones may hold their breaths until the end, when they become unconscious from oxygen deprivation. It can be quite alarming to see this happening, but it does not pose any danger to your child. Your child will recover quickly and no lasting harm can be done.

Most commonly, these tantrums occur between the age of 1 and 3 years. Your child will be going through major developmental periods during this period. Everything is unfamiliar to your child. They may be learning new ways to interact in the world. This is also the age when autonomy is becoming a reality. Your child is now able to see that they are an independent person. Your child wants interaction and to do so much but cannot communicate. You might see them impulsively doing something they do not want, such as jumping off a counter. If you stop them, it can lead to an argument. They have difficulty understanding why you say "no" at this stage and feel overwhelmed by the feelings of disappointment, anger and anger that follow.

Reasons to Tantrums

Your Child Wants Something

Most often, a tantrum occurs because your child is envious of something. It is possible that they want something that they are unable to have at the moment. They throw a huge tantrum over it. Perhaps they want an Ice Cream cone for breakfast. They throw a major fit, because they are angry and disappointed.

Your Child Doesn't Need Anything

Sometimes, the tantrum is caused by an unmet needs. They may feel tired, hungry, thirsty, and in desperate need of diaper changes. They want something but are having trouble communicating it. If the child doesn't understand what they need, they may cry or become frustrated.

Your Child Wants to Avoid Something

Sometimes the tantrum is caused to avoidance. The tantrum may be caused by your child trying to get him or her to do something they do not want to. Instead of accepting the fact as it is, your child starts to cry and scream. Perhaps it is bedtime and your child is screaming at you about being in the crib. Your child is seeking autonomy in this situation and is trying their best to be independent.

Your Child Wants Attention

Sometimes, a toddler will get upset if you're not paying enough attention. This is because toddlers are taught that even negative attention can be better than no attention. If you haven't been giving your child all the attention that he/she needs, there is a chance your child might throw a fit just to get your attention.

Your Child Can't Communicate
Sometimes, the cause of a tantrum is just not being capable of communicating needs and wants. These are big feelings your child isn't yet able to handle and can turn into an explosive situation.

Parent's Guide on Dealing with Tantrums
These are some of the things you should keep in mind when you deal with tantrums. The child's ability to respond to tantrums will decide how they learn to manage them. You have to be able and willing in your own self-regulation to help your child learn to manage his/her emotions. You set the stage for how your child will respond to tantrums and how they can be handled. Here are some tips to

help you deal with tantrum-prone children:

It's okay not to be mad. It is normal to feel stressed if you hear your child screaming. It is a normal biological reaction. Your biological predisposition is to try and stop your child from screaming. Be aware that it's normal to be upset. But, that doesn't mean you have to lose your temper.

Keep taking a deep inhale: Before you get started with dealing with your child, make sure to remember to take a deep and long breath. This will help clear your head and prevent from making mistakes or regretting them later. In this way, you can teach your child skills in self-regulation that will help him or her to deal with the situation later.

Your child is having a hard moment. Parents may ask why their children behave like this. This is the wrong way of looking at it. Your child isn't trying to be difficult, he/she is just having a hard moment and the only way to handle those intense, overwhelming emotions is through a tantrum.

Find out why your child is having a tantrum. You can avoid common triggers such as tiredness or hunger, so you can recognize them and take steps to prevent future tantrums. You can make naptime sacred to your child and make sure you don't leave until it is absolutely necessary.

Don't worry if you don't have children. If you haven't, then it is possible that your children are too young for these types of tantrums. Most children will have some type of public meltdown sometime in their lives. Parents know what you are going though, so they can help you. They feel your frustration and anger. Do not be embarrassed if you receive a rude stare, comment, or even a slap on the face when your child throws a fit. It happens. It's normal. It is important not to let other people distract from you or make yourself feel bad. You could end up struggling.

Redirection to reduce tantrums

You have one of the most important skills as a parent: the ability to redirect from a tantrum. This is especially true when dealing with a child who is very young.

Children that are having a tantrum are usually throwing a fit due to the fact that their emotional side of their brains is on auto-pilot. Your child has the ability think in a rational, calm way and can also think emotionally. We all have this ability. Our emotional side can run wild and take control of the situation. This is a sign that we are not making wise decisions. We act in impulsive ways, which can often lead us to other problems. Unintended consequences can be a result of our decisions, which we may not have anticipated.

If these same behaviors can be exhibited by adults, it should not surprise you that they can also happen to your child. These moments when the child is overwhelmed by emotions, they have trouble thinking rationally. During these periods, the child's emotional side is likely to take over and overwhelm their thoughts and actions. This is what happens in tantrums. Your child is likely feeling overwhelming, strong emotions. It's possible that he/she does not know how best to handle them.

It is possible to engage with your child's rational side even if they are having tantrums. Redirection is exactly what this will allow you to do. You will attempt to do or speak something that will make the child's logical mind stop and pay attention. You want the logical brain to engage and control the individual.

There are many things you can do to redirect your child's attention. To get them off their tracks, you can show them something different than what they are currently looking at. You will see this happen with infants. If they cry, you can shake a rattle before them. Or you could offer a pacifier and a bottle. Some people quit trying to redirect their children after the toddler years. People stop trying redirect their children as they feel that their older children can better cope with the changes of growing up. But, your tactics for infants are no different from those used with toddlers still learning to navigate. It will take some time, effort and skill.

Redirection can occur in many ways. Primarily, though, the goal is the same: you will redirect from a bad situation into a good one in some form or another. Let's assume your toddler knocked down his blocks the third time. Now he is having a fit. He kicked at them and threw one across. You can change the direction by trying something different or doing something completely else. It is possible to say, for instance, "Throwing block hurts people". We don't toss blocks. Your child is not being reprimanded. You are not trying to shame or punish your child. Instead, you calmly try to redirect his or her focus. You are trying convincing your child, with your already limited attention span and using the language of calmness, that there are better options.

Chapter 14: Discipline Without Shame

Embarrassement is the worst form of discipline for children. They will act out yet again to restore balance and attempt to regain their dignity. It is important to recognize this and to find ways to discipline children without shame. Your discipline should remain reasonable, clear, and understandable by your children.

Establishing rules and guidelines is the first step. It is essential that your child understands "Thus Far and No More." Make sure you do it in a time when you aren't punishing but when things are calm. You are simply explaining to your child what is happening.

If your child is acting out, don't get mad at them. Take some time to reflect and then respond to the actions. Be calm, talk with them, and try not to punish them because you are angry or frustrated. You can often end up discharging them poorly when they lash out in anger.

Talk to the child using a perspective of "I", "me", and not "Mommy", "Daddy". They should feel that it is a personal offence to do something. That is why you are giving them the discipline. They must be able interact with and relate to you.

For some kids, time is a very humiliating consequence. This is especially true if they are surrounded by their siblings. Other consequences are possible for such children. These consequences will allow them to learn without feeling shameful. Natural consequences are the best, because your toddler is likely to learn quickly from their mistakes even if they have terrible natural consequences.

No matter what type of punishment is used, it's important to show love to your child. They don't need to feel embarrassed or ashamed of themselves. The goal is to make them realize that wrong choices can have serious consequences. Be kind and loving. Tell them that you love them and that you will correct their bad behavior.

Chapter 15: Things You Need to Consider When Disciplining Toddlers

Parents can attest that raising a toddler is difficult. These tiny bundles are a joy to behold, but can also become stubborn children that test the patience limits and will often cause problems for their parents.

It is also a phase in childhood where they can assert their independence. It is the phase in which they start to speak their first words. "No," is a sign of their determination to follow their lead. They love running away from home to escape. Normal toddlers have a lot of energy. They love to run and jump and play, explore and discover all that interests. They love the touch and explore with all their senses. They can become impulsive, so toddlers may be clumsy or touch things. The parents must teach their children how safe it is to touch or handle hot objects.

While raising a child as a toddler requires a lot of work, it is worth the effort. The toddler stage is a time of rapid developmental change. It is essential to provide a disciplined approach that encourages independence as well as teaches socially responsible behavior.

Parents often assume that parenting techniques will be the same for all kids. Every child has a unique set of traits. They are part and parcel of the genetic code that each child inherits from his parents. Some toddlers have shy personalities, others are calm and even-tempered. Others are outgoing and can be aggressive.

To help the child adjust to the outside world, it is important that you understand their personality and natural behavior. Be sure to respect your toddler's unique personality. For their mental, emotional, and social development, it is crucial to provide adequate care and nourishment.

A. Temperament, Behavior

Temperament can be described as the genetically and biologically influenced core that influences the style and response of an individual. The temperament of a child is often a predictor of their adult temperament.

The child's behavior is a result of his temperament, his cognitive, emotional, as well as physical development. It is influenced and influenced by the child's beliefs about himself, other people, and the world. It is an inborn characteristic, but there are many ways to help your toddler make it work for him.

Nine dimensions or traits relate to temperament

Activity levels are the physical activity that your toddler engages in while doing some activities. It also includes the inactive periods.

* Is your child a wanderer? Can they not sit still or move about all the time?

* Is your toddler an independent, quiet child who loves to watch TV or play by themselves?

Rhythmicity describes the predictability, or unpredictability, of physical and biologic functions such as sleep, hunger, and bowel movements.

* Does your child like routines and regular eating?
* Does the man display an unpredictability and dislike for routine?

To stay focused for a specific period of time, you need to be able to focus and maintain attention.

* Does your toddler keep their hands off the task at hand?
* Is he easily frustrated?

The initial response (Approach or Withdrawal), is the way that something new and unknown affects you. It is the first reaction they have to a stimulus. This could be a person, place, food, or toy. The expressions they make or the mood they are in, as well as facial expressions such smiles or motor activity (e.g reaching for a food toy or chewing on it), show their reaction. Negative reactions can include withdrawal, crying or fussing, pushing away, and spitting.

* Is he wary about unfamiliar situations or strangers, or is he averse to them?

* Does he enjoy meeting new people?

The intensity of a reaction to any event or circumstance is directly related to its level. The reactions of toddlers to events are different. Some respond with happiness, some laugh, and others are unable to react.

* Do your children always react to something you say?

* Does your child display his emotions in a clear way?

Adaptability means that a child can adapt to change.

* Is your child able to adjust to sudden changes or disruptions of his routine and plans?

* Does he find it hard to accept changes and resist them as much as possible?

Distractibility refers the child's willingness/inability to be distracted. It refers the outside stimulus's effects on your child's behavior.

* Your child's ability to focus on his task despite distractions

* Can he concentrate when there are people and other activities happening in the environment

Your child's understanding and perception of the world will determine his mood. Some children feel happy and accept others have a negative reaction.

* Does he constantly display mood swings?
* Does he tend to be happy?

Sensory Threshold relates to your sensitivity for sensory stimulation. Sensitive children to stimulation require careful and gradual introduction to other people, experiences, or objects.

* Does your child find loud or bright sounds, bright lights, and/or food textures irritating?
* Does he feel completely at peace with these things and would he be open to them as such?

There are 3 main types of toddlers.

* Active Toddlers or Feisty Toddlers. These children are active and energetic, and they can be seen moving around, kicking, and even inside their mothers' uterus. They

crawl and move as infants. To get rid of their energy, toddlers climb, jump, fidget, and run a lot. They may get anxious or excited by new situations or strangers.

They are joyful, lively, and naturally energetic. But they will be very vocal if they are not happy. These toddlers can be very stubborn, making it difficult for you to get your routines in order.

To help him succeed

Recognize and understand your triggers.

Teaching them self-help skills is a great way to motivate them if they're feeling tired, or to calm down if the activity level is high. You can calm yourself down by taking deep, slow, easy breaths, counting from one to 10, and doing jumping jacks. This will help you get rid of any excess energy and allow you to redirect them to other activities.

Create a daily routine for them that includes play as well as other activities that will improve their grossmotor movements. You should give them opportunities to explore and have fun. It is vital to childproof your property.

Take a break from work and allow your child to sleep. A good afternoon nap can help prevent mood swings from escalating into tantrums.

Do not allow your children to sit still in front of the TV, or to engage in passive behaviors. Let them go outside to have fun and break boredom.

Become a calming influence. You can help them understand how their temperament affects their temperament.

* Passive Toddlers or Cautious Toddlers. These children enjoy activities that don't require a lot, are slower and like to sit down more often. They take longer to adjust to new situations, are slower to meet people and withdraw from situations. They also require ample time to complete their tasks.

B. B.

Discipline is a problem for many parents, especially new ones. Parents are searching for ways to raise positive and well-mannered children capable of facing the real world.

There is no right or correct approach to disciplining children. Find the right discipline method to match your child's personality and behavior.

These simple methods are popular among parents all over the globe.

Encouragement & Commendation

Good behavior is encouraged by encouraging words and praise. When your child does something admirable, give them small rewards or praise to encourage them to improve. You can praise them for good behaviours and encourage them to do it again and again.

Rethinking

Many times, positive reactions can be obtained by changing your tone or reframing your thoughts. Instead of giving instructions such as "don't" or "get," try reorganizing your strategy to reflect a solicitation. It is better to use the phrases, "wouldn't you...if it was fine with me?"

Remember that your toddler does not have to be like you. It is important to think about things from his perspective. For example, if your son doesn't want to ride in the child car seats, you can say, "I know that you really love sitting in your car seat. But, it is essentially similar to this seat belt that my husband has." They make us both safer." By this you are showing your son how safe it is to use the proper tools.

Disregard

You can signal your child by not paying attention to tantrums or fits in an intentional way that you aren't affected and won't give in to his desires. To make this more effective, other adults in the house must be aware of the strategy for disciplining and breaking the child's tantrum behaviors. It might seem harsh but this is how you curb your child's anger. If your child is doing something naughty in an attempt to get you attention, you can help him by looking away or ignoring him. Do not meet his eyes, glare, and get angry. He will know that you are paying attention. His behavior should not be disturbed. He should not see you screaming or throwing tantrums to get your attention.

Break

It's also known as a Time-out. This is a popular method that parents used to discipline their children. The idea behind it is to place him in a "cozy spot", a safe, quiet area of your home. There he will reflect on what he did. It is essential that you have access to him, and make sure he is safe. After the break is over, have a discussion about what happened. Let him explain his actions and give you time.

A good rule to follow when setting a time limit for your child is that it must be equal in length to their age. For instance, if your son or daughter is 2 years, then give him a two-minute break. You should use this method sparingly so that your child does not feel isolated.

Substitutes and Distraction

Try to distract your child before he gets into the habit of hitting something in the house. It is possible to get his attention by giving him something. Young children are easily distracted as they often have a short attention span. You can also swap his toys for something more stimulating.

Toddlers may not be able to comprehend why they are being disciplined. Keep his attention on something else. You can grab his attention by calling his name. Then, once his eyes are fixed on you, show it to him something that will motivate him to follow you.

Conclusion

I hope that you find this book useful in helping you deal with your growing child. The toddler stage, which is more talked about than the teenage years, is what parents refer to as the worst. It doesn't have be this way. As you know, there are many changes happening as your baby turns into a toddler. It's no surprise toddlers can sometimes be moody. It is up you, the parent, to provide your toddler with the patience he or she deserves.

Parents are the best witnesses to their child's developmental milestones. It's not easy to know where to draw the line. There are many things you may not notice, or forget to tell your doctor. Some parents see milestones not as important. There is nothing to worry because they did just fine and didn't have to worry about whether they were reading, talking, or walking. They believe in letting Nature take its course.

Yes, it is true. However, did you know that children born to parents with a development disability have a greater chance of recovery if their disability was detected and managed early? You shouldn't feel guilty for not having detected a problem sooner. This is why developmental landmarks are used as a guideline, so parents know when something's wrong.

You don't have to be frustrated by a child who struggles at something. Your intuition and gut are your best friends.

If you still have concerns, consult a child specialist and share your worries. If there's something wrong, you have a chance for recovery. If not, your mind can rest easy.

Your child always comes first. It doesn't matter whether you're at home, at work or out at the grocery, if you have to spend the time teaching your toddler the right and wrong ways to behave, that's okay. Do not worry about being judged by other parents. It doesn't matter if other parents judge you.

You have to nurture your child's brain as your toddler grows. You can learn about your child's cognitive stages and how to help him/her learn self-regulation. You'll be able to raise a strong-willed person with unconditional Love and Discipline. You're going raise a child capable of self-discipline. You will see your child grow up confident, ready to tackle the world and believe they can succeed in whatever career they choose. Your child will be proud of his or her accomplishments, and you will love him regardless of the circumstances. As with raising a child, there will always be challenges. No matter how happy your kid is, there will still be times when he or she is angry, frustrated, or sad. There will be times that you're angry at your child. It is inevitable. Take the good times and the hard times as a parent. Then, learn to be a competent parent.

Your child must be able comprehend everything they see, hear, touch, and feel. Children must be able connect things or they will lose faith in themselves. They will become frustrated when they are unable to understand the world. All they want is to survive in adulthood. You have probably ever stopped to imagine what it must be like to be a toddler with all the adults around you. Think about how your toddler might feel if they need a break from you after a long day. Your needs may be understood by you, and you're aware of how important adult relationships can be, but your child doesn't. They aren't clear on where their needs come from. While it is easy for you to call your friend while your kid is sleeping, you are unable to communicate with them. They need help in their transition. They need help understanding that everyone feels exactly the same way. They need help to understand how to express their emotions correctly and communicate their desires, needs, and emotions.

It is also important to assess each child's needs. Some babies born prematurely have a harder time reaching certain milestones. They will not develop as quickly as a fullterm baby. Stop playing games with your baby. Let them enjoy this moment as it is.

Perhaps your child's personality or temperament is responsible for their delayed growth. Their temperament and personality may be the reason they are not enthusiastic about something. This doesn't necessarily mean that they have a developmental delay. For example, expecting a child who is naturally shy to socialize with other children or play with them like them doesn't signify that they have a developmental delay. It is simply that the child's personality doesn't match what they do.

If you are still unsure about what you should or shouldn't do, where to look for delays, and how to plan ahead for their developmental milestones, you can use this comprehensive guide. This guide will provide all the information necessary to keep track of their physical, cognitive, sensory, and speech development. Be a responsible, good parent and make sure you use it carefully.

www.ingramcontent.com/pod-product-compliance
Lightning Source LLC
Chambersburg PA
CBHW071844080526
44589CB00012B/1107